234

INVITATION TO HOLINESS

INVITATION TO HOLINESS

JAMES C. FENHAGEN

1817

Harper & Row, Publishers, San Francisco

Cambridge, Hagerstown, New York, Philadelphia
London, Mexico City, São Paulo, Singapore, Sydney

FIRST EDITION

Library of Congress Cataloging-in-Publication Data
Fenhagen, James C.
    Invitation to holiness.

    1. Holiness.   2. Christian life—1960—
    I. Title.
BT767.F38   1985   234'8   85–42774
ISBN 0-06-062351-9

85 86 87 88 89 HC 10 9 8 7 6 5 4 3 2 1

For Eulalie,
and for Leila, Jim, and John,
in thanksgiving

Contents

Introduction   ix

1. Wholeness and Beyond   3
2. The Roots of Holiness   15
3. The Holy Person in Contemporary Society   27
4. Pastoral Dimensions of Holiness   39
5. Prayer and the Kingdom Vision   53
6. Work, Vocation, and Integrity   65
7. Education for Holiness   75

Epilogue: A Modern Parable   85
Notes   93
Index   96

Introduction

At the heart of Christian life and ministry stands the call for one person to care for another. To care for others—indeed, to care deeply about the world in which we live—is to share in the ministry of Jesus Christ. Caring, therefore, is not simply a sentiment, but rather a way of actively using our lives on behalf of others. Caring involves us in a very personal way with other human beings, but it also involves us in impersonal ways with the attitudes and structures that shape both individuals and societies. Although we speak of it quite readily, caring is not easy, nor do we care for others without cost to ourselves.

In the pages that follow, I would like to explore the ministry of caring—which is, of course, what we mean when we speak of pastoral care—not in the context of the psychological disciplines through which we normally view human behavior, but in the context of what the Bible speaks of as the vision of holiness—a vision intimately linked with Jesus' teaching about the Kingdom of God.

In an article in *Pastoral Psychology* Don Browning, professor of religion and psychological studies at the University of Chicago Divinity School, speaks with some passion about the readiness of the Church to let what is essentially a theological understanding of human nature give way to whatever seems to be current on the psychological scene.

We have made advances in our technologies of intervention into such life cycle issues as adolescence, sexuality, marriage, adulthood, aging and death, but our normative theological visions of these milestones of the life cycle have received less and less of our attention. More and more, I fear, we have tried to intervene with these life cycle issues with increasingly diffuse and confused normative theological images. We have borrowed from the psychotherapeutic and developmental psychologies, but we are sometimes oblivious to the fact that we appropriate from them not only scientific information and therapeutic techniques but various normative visions of human fulfillment which are neither philosophically sound nor theologically defensible.[1]

In the last few years a number of scholars have taken up Browning's challenge and sought to reexamine the fields of pastoral care and religious education with his critique in mind.[2] My aim in this book is not so much to respond to Browning's critique as it is to offer a "normative vision of human fulfillment" that is theologically based as well as psychologically sound. A view of humanity that begins with the self is by definition limited simply because, from the biblical perspective, we can never speak of self apart from our relation to other selves.

Whenever we speak of human growth and development someone, somewhere, has an outcome in mind. We speak of growing toward maturity, and even as we speak our words and concepts are shaped by whatever images of maturity it is that we hold. We speak of self-actualization and wholeness, but not without some specific understandings of the nature of humanity and human growth in mind. These are not issues unrelated to the Christian faith. In Jesus Christ we have an image of what humanity is about—an image that we must interpret in the light of the total Gospel vision.

To help develop the vision, I want to examine a very ancient—and sometimes misconstrued—word in the biblical tradition. The word is "holiness," which in its most simple definition means to be touched or encompassed by the glory of God. Holiness, I would like to suggest, offers a vision of human fulfillment that is worth our attention. "Strive for peace with all people," we read in the Letter to the Hebrews, "and for the holiness without which no one will see the Lord" (12:14). This is ancient thought with contemporary implications.

In the chapters that follow I will seek to explore what this word from Scripture might mean, both in the way we see ourselves, and in the way we care for others. Behind the calm exteriors that we present to one another lie untold stories of human struggle and pain. I believe profoundly that people need space and support in dealing with those inner conflicts that only they in the last analysis can deal with, and the movement of their journeys needs to be responded to with respect and care. But journeys have destinations, and a human life in the sight of God is a life with meaning and purpose. It is my conviction that the biblical idea of holiness, stripped of some of the accretions that it has acquired over the centuries, is a word that speaks very much to our contemporary situation. It is a word that includes the idea of wholeness, but in a larger context. The issue, I believe, is not an unimportant one. Unless we are clear about who we are and what we are about, we can very easily embark on a journey that has us marching to the wrong tune.

I will begin with that quest for wholeness that is so fundamental to human growth, and will seek to place this quest in a larger context—that is, in the context of the biblical vision of holiness. In Chapters 2 and 3, we shall examine the idea of holiness and its implications for pastoral care and everyday life. Chapters 4, 5, and 6 look at some of the fruits of holiness as these relate to our inner and outer journeys, and Chapter 7 examines how the vision of which we speak can be communicated to others.

"Strive for peace with all people, and for the holiness without which no one will see the Lord." I would be so bold as to suggest that it is only in "seeing the Lord" that we come to see ourselves as we were created to be, and to experience this is to experience the holiness of God.

This book, like many others, is the product of the interaction I have experienced with many people over the past ten years. I am particularly indebted to Christ Church, St. Luke's, and St. Mark's Episcopal Church in San Antonio, Texas; to the Episcopal Dioceses of Atlanta, Southern Virginia, and Pennsylvania; and to the 1984 Christian Education Conference at Kanuga in Hendersonville, North Carolina, which invited me to present portions of this material as it was being developed.

And finally, I would like to thank Helen Jones for her wise critique; John Koenig for his encouragement; and Elizabeth Hasen and Karen Armington, not only for typing the many drafts of this book but for supplying thoughtful and helpful comments along the way.

Wholeness and Beyond

1.

Morris West, in his novel *The Shoes of the Fisherman*, offered the following description of what it meant to be a human being. For a period in my life it served as a significant image in my own self-understanding. The description comes from what West portrays as the secret journal of Pope Kyril I, a prototype of Pope John XXIII. Kyril writes:

Yesterday I met a whole man. It is a rare experience, but always an illuminating one. It costs so much to be a full human being that there are very few who have the enlightenment, or the courage, to pay the price. . . . One has to abandon altogether the search for security, and reach out to the risk of living with full arms. One has to embrace the world like a lover, and yet demand no easy return of love. One has to accept pain as a condition of existence. One has to court doubt and darkness as the cost of knowing. One needs a will stubborn in conflict, but apt to the total consequence of living and dying.[1]

We have here in West's description an eloquent picture of human wholeness, masculine in tone but relevant to us all. It echoes a strong voice in contemporary society in which the search for personal fulfillment and wholeness are dominant themes. West's description is seductive because it appeals to all that is heroic in Western secular culture—and I might add, because I am part of this culture, to all that is heroic in me. What is not reflected is the basic alienation in all of us. Because it separates us from God, this alienation makes it impossible for us to be the kind of person West describes, apart from God's initiative in us and in the world.

THE QUEST FOR WHOLENESS

For the Christian, the quest for wholeness is very much a part of our journey in Christ. Therefore, because wholeness means so many things to so many people, it is important for us to be clear about what we actually mean. When psychologist Carl Jung began to speak of the quest for wholeness as the fundamental movement toward growth in the human personality, he provided a new point of meeting between psychology and religion. In the movement toward individuation, which is fundamental to the maturing process, Jung wrote that we are energized by the presence of Self in each of us which draws all the opposing and contributing forces within us toward ultimate wholeness. Unlike West's description of the solitary hero, Jung's understanding of human growth invites us to participate in a process in which we become partners with the divine Spirit in the universal movement toward the fulfillment of our humanity.

The question we as Christians must ask, however, is this: How do we draw on the insights of the human sciences without distorting what is unique about the Gospel? Because we live in an age where the psychological disciplines offer the dominant images by which we understand ourselves, there is a strong tendency to take what are essentially psychological insights and make them fit our theological framework, even when they don't. A case in point is the often-heard equation of "wholeness" with the word "salvation," where it is noted that wholeness and salvation seem to have a common root. In fact, however, salvation and wholeness are quite different things. Salvation is a biblical word referring to our deliverance from sin and its consequences and the coming of peace and reconciliation with God. Wholeness, as it is most often used today, is essentially psychological in meaning. It suggests completion—the resolution of opposites or, in another context, the absence of disease. The differences are more than semantic. Salvation does not depend on wholeness, but rather on the self-offering of Jesus Christ on the Cross, in which even our alienation and brokenness are used for God's purposes.

We live in a world that is desperate for self-understanding and growth, but only if it can be assured that what we buy can reduce the anxiety that so many feel. Whoever promises such relief at low personal cost will find ready consumers. From the point of view of

the Gospel, hwoever, such relief is temporary at best. More is required than what we can do for ourselves. The truth that sets us
free is the fruit of faith and responsiveness to what God has done
because we are unable to save ourselves. If we take Christian theology seriously, it becomes obvious that the insights of psychology cannot automatically be affirmed as tenets of the Christian
faith. What is needed is a capacity to draw a truth from wherever it
comes, using the Christian revelation as the place in which we
stand to determine what is of ultimate value.

In the same vein we must honestly ask whether or not the Jungian concept of the Self can be equated with the Christian doctrine
of God or what is meant by life in Christ, without seriously diminishing the radical nature of the Christian understanding of redemption. This is not in any way to demean the profound insights
of Jungian psychology or, for that matter, the insights of Freudian
thought, but rather to question the often uncritical way in which
we adapt the Christian faith to current psychological dogma, to
the diminishment of both. Twenty-five years ago the trend in popular religious circles was to seek to explain Christianity in Freudian terms, and many thoughtful people in the Church today feel
that Freudian thought is more compatible with the Christian doctrine of the Incarnation than are the sometimes transpersonal reflections of Dr. Jung. The point is that truth is truth from wherever
it comes; but without a place to stand, it is difficult to determine
what is ultimately life-giving and what is not.

In recent years Christian education has been very much influenced by some of the creative work being done by developmental
psychologists. Building on the pioneer work of Jean Piaget and
Erik Erikson, significant research has been done in child and adult
development, moral development, and most recently, in the work
of James Fowler, faith development. Of particular interest is the
work of Carol Gilligan in the field of adult development and her
response to her colleague Lawrence Kohlberg, in which she argues for the uniqueness in the way women develop as "moral persons."[2] In my own thinking I have drawn from much of this material, often quite uncritically, although admittedly always with a

slight uneasiness about the way life is supposed to fit into such clearly defined categories.

In a brilliant analysis of current developmental theory Gabriel Moran, the dean of the School of Christian Education at New York University, asks (as a friendly critic), "Is it possible to imagine some facets of life as proceeding in some other way than pushing relentlessly upward and forward to bigger things?" He then comments:

I am deeply interested in the imagery that is presupposed by theories of development. I am concerned with finding imagery that allows people to resist a premature closure of what their lives mean. The great religious traditions probably cannot be said to have theories of human development, but they do insist that an answer must eventually be given, and they do have images and practices that embody a meaning of life as a whole.[3]

It is my increasing conviction that we have in those images associated with the Christian idea of holiness at least one answer that needs to be explored, for in the idea of holiness we have indeed a vision of what life is about.

FINDING OUR CENTER IN CHRIST

In an interesting book offered as a contribution toward the dialogue between East and West, John A.T. Robinson noted the difference between the center and the edges of the human psyche.[4] Most of us, he points out, seem to be more concerned with strengthening our boundaries than with developing our center. We let our edges become hard and brittle, or we barricade them in defense against new ideas or new relationships, and at the same time we leave our centers relatively unattended. The quest for wholeness has to do with softening our edges and strengthening our center, which for the Christian involves entering more deeply into the relationship offered to us in Christ. When our edges are soft, we are able to cross boundaries into worlds different from our own and respond creatively to ideas and situations that otherwise would be experienced only as threat.

The pathway to wholeness, therefore, involves on the one hand bringing to consciousness the inner conflicts that prevent us from owning our own worth, while on the other hand claiming the gift of faith that makes it possible for us to enter into that relationship with the Christ through whom our worth is assured.

WHAT IS HIDDEN SHALL COME TO LIGHT

In a provocative passage in St. Matthew's Gospel, Jesus speaks of the necessity of bringing to light our often deeply held beliefs about our relationship to him, so that they might be tested and thereby expanded, even if this means facing misunderstanding from those around us. "So have no fear of them," Jesus says, "for nothing is covered that will not be revealed, or hidden that will not be known" (10:26).

All of us carry within us aspects of our own selves that we would rather not have known—aspects of ourselves that we often deny—because the threat of exposure seems too powerful. The invitation Jesus offers to us is a relationship that casts out fear, making it possible for us to dare expose our vulnerability to ourselves and others. As Paul affirms so confidently, "If God is for us, who can be against us?" (Rom. 8:31).

In my own life, like so many people I know, I have struggled to become sufficiently aware of those inner conflicts that distort my vision, so that the way I act might more nearly reflect what I say and who it is I understand myself to be. This is what I understand the quest for wholeness to be about; it is not something arrived at easily, if at all. But because wholeness has to do with our freedom from inner fear, and therefore with our freedom to act, it is critical to the life in Christ.

There is tremendous power in self-discovery. When the inner conflicts that blur our vision are brought to consciousness, power is released that enables us to make choices about what our lives are for. What blocks these choices are the many "oughts" and the many hidden fears that cause us to harden our edges and avoid dealing with those aspects of our lives that nourish our center.

After thirty years in the ministry I am just beginning to realize how much of my identity as a priest has been shaped by those many "oughts" that I have collected over the years as a way of dealing with feelings of inadequacy. For a long time the only energy for prayer that I could summon was energy that came in response to an inner construct that told me I "ought" to pray and how. This is far different from the energy we experience when the thirst for prayer comes from our center. The first reflects inner conflict; the second, freedom to move with the Spirit.

One of the difficulties many couples experience in marriage is the recognition—sometimes after many years—that the covenant they have made is not to each other but to the *institution* of marriage, with all the "oughts" that this conveys. When we are able to live out of the center of our lives with edges soft enough to adapt to change, we discover that it is not marriage that we marry, but another human being. And often this discovery is not made until the pain of brokenness brings what is often a deep and unrecognized conflict to light.

When I think of wholeness in my own life, I think of a finely tuned orchestra in which each instrument, guided by the conductor, contributes its part toward a magnificent symphony of sound. There are times—and in recent years, increasing times—when I have heard this sound and I know that I am in tune with the Spirit of God who moves within me. Sometimes the sound is discordant, even harsh, but it is nonetheless one sound. This is wholeness. It can include themes of joy and themes of pain, but there is still one sound. This is very different from what happens when the instruments that represent the many-faceted aspects of my personality are playing in opposition to each other. When this happens, I experience inner chaos and confusion—the very opposite of wholeness. The answer is not to play louder, nor to pretend we do not hear, but rather to take time to listen to the many sounds so that the message they contain can be brought to light. The inner freedom the Gospel promises is experienced when our identity in Christ is honored and trusted and nourished. It is experienced when our inner lives are in tune, not in the sense of having arrived, but rather in the sense of being able to hear and respond to the themes and rhythms that the Spirit offers in calling us out of ourselves. The journey in Christ is a journey shaped by the biblical story of salvation in which is embodied a will to holiness.

Wholeness, when open to the Spirit of God, is a seedbed for holiness. When our center has been re-formed in Christ, an environment is created that opens us to the promptings of the Kingdom. In biblical terms, like Bartimaeus we begin to see.

The issue, I believe, is a critical one. Without the vision of holiness that Jesus embodies firmly planted in our consciousness, wholeness can turn inwards; and instead of our world expanding, it contracts—even as we use the language and forms of faith.

I believe we have to ask ourselves in all honesty why, for so many Christians (and I include myself), it is so hard to act on those aspects of our faith that challenge the status quo. In response to the critical issues that face the world, we seem to be better at talking than acting—and as a result, much of what people see and hear of the Christian faith is often a religion of narrow focus and brittle edges.

WHOLENESS, HOLINESS, AND THE GIFT OF FAITH

The Christian faith is more than good feeling or even inward support, although at times both of these are present. The Christian faith is a clearly articulated vision of reality based on the way human beings have experienced God's action in history. It is incredibly realistic about the power of human sin and affirms that until there is a basic reorientation in the way we think and the way we see and the way we live, the incredible destructiveness we see in the world will continue. Christianity is not a religion that sees the human journey primarily in terms of growth (which implies a natural unfolding), but in terms of transformation (which implies a radical restructuring of the center of our being). Christianity is not fundamentally about wholeness, but holiness.

Holiness, I admit, is not a word that fits comfortably in everyday conversation. For most people, holiness—if it means anything at all—connotes an other-worldliness either so much out of the reach of the average person that it is not even thought of as a possibility, or else so offbeat as to be not even desirable.

Holiness, as many of us have probably discovered, is not an easy word to drop into conversation. The situation reminds me of the time when my daughter, as a very young child, went on a visit to Savannah, Georgia. Her grandmother made a great point of taking her to the birthplace of Juliet Lowe, who founded the Girl Scouts. "Now," my mother-in-law pointed out to her young charge, "if anyone asks you who founded the Girl Scouts, you can tell them." A year later, when my daughter was with her grandmother again, she presented her with a pregnant dilemma. "Mama," she said, "no one has ever asked me who founded the Girl Scouts!" Talking about holiness presents us with a similar problem.

Holiness, in one strand of biblical understanding, is closely associated with Jesus' teaching about the Kingdom of God. It is not concerned so much with accumulating desirable attributes that we call holy, as it is with the way we perceive reality and the way we act on these perceptions. Holiness, therefore, is a political word. A holy person is a person who sees the world, if only momentarily, through the eyes of Christ and is drawn to act in response to this vision.

The Christian life involves more than growth and development. It involves conversion and transformation, a radical turning of the Self toward the God who made us and who continues to sustain us. Christian faith is about an inner transformation of consciousness resulting from our encounter with the living Christ. "I have been crucified with Christ," proclaimed the Apostle Paul, "it is no longer I who live, but Christ who lives in me" (Gal. 2:20). "When anyone is united to Christ, there is a new world: the old order has gone, and a new order has already begun" (2 Cor. 5:17). The Christian revelation promises a radical vision of what it means to be a human being. The life in Christ does not change the way we look, nor does it eliminate our peculiarities or the results of our own brokenness and estrangement. What it does do is open us to the Spirit of God in ways that increase in us the capacity for love. The fruit of conversion is a life that can be used by God for the healing of the world.

In her collection of letters the novelist Flannery O'Connor bears witness to the importance of coming to terms with the substance of the Christian revelation, not as an intellectual exercise but as an expression of faith.

For me, dogma is only a gateway to contemplation and an instrument of freedom and not of restriction. It preserves mystery for the human mind. [A mystery, I would add, which the search for wholeness by itself can never solve or fully understand.] When I ask myself how I know I believe I have no satisfactory answer at all, no assurance at all. . . . I can only say with Peter, Lord, I believe, help my unbelief. And all I can say about my love of God is, Lord, help me in my lack of it.[5]

No triumphalism here—only a mind both rooted in and enlightened by the Christian faith and, as a result, open to the mystery of God who is in all things, yet beyond all things. The pastoral task of the Church is to raise up men and women who can walk with one another as they struggle to find wholeness in their lives. But it is also in the business of nourishing holiness in the midst of our experiences of brokenness and wholeness, knowing that in so doing we nourish also the gift of faith. Faith opens us to the mystery of God in all of its manifestations—in the world, and in those people with whom we share this planet. Faith draws us into worlds other than our own. It invites us to see that dimension of reality that is just beyond our sight. It presents us not with a goal, but with a vision that remains forever open ended.

At the conclusion of Walker Percy's novel *The Second Coming*, Will Barrett encounters an old priest made memorable by a bad eye that seemed to spin as you looked at him. In a desperate attempt to find some degree of wholeness in his life, Barrett grasps the aging priest hoping to find the answer—or maybe the question—that continues to elude him. After a moment he backs away as the words form in his consciousness. "Could it be," he says to himself, "that the Lord is here masquerading behind this simple holy face?"[6]

As I read these words I too wondered, and I asked myself, was what Will Barrett saw a vision of holiness, or only sentimental longing? And if it was indeed holiness that he experienced, what in reality, if anything, does it mean?

The Roots of Holiness

2.

When Will Barrett describes the countenance of Father Weatherbee as holy, he is drawing on the cumulative religious experience of humankind reaching back to the beginning of recorded time. Holiness in human life is a reflection of the holiness of God and, therefore, has always been associated with religious experience. Holiness is a special word that suggests not so much a particular quality of the divine, as the essence of that transcendent mystery which for the believer stands at the center of human existence. The word holiness carries with it connotations of the numinous, and therefore includes the experience of awe and wonder and power—all of which cannot be clearly defined. Holiness always implies something more—pointing to that mystery which can never be contained. More than any other word in the history of language, it speaks of the essence of religious experience.

"And the Lord spoke to Moses and said, 'Speak to all the community of the Israelites in these words: You shall be holy, because I, the Lord your God, am holy' " (Lev. 19:1–4). This simple injunction describes the essential nature of God's covenant with his creation. It is a description not only of God, but of humanity created in God's image. To speak of holiness as a human possibility, therefore, is to say something quite specific about what it means to be human. We are saying that we cannot fully understand ourselves apart from the way we understand God.

HOLINESS IN THE BIBLE

In the account of the call of Moses recorded in the Book of Exodus there are intimations of God's holiness which make this passage a core description of human religious experience. As Moses is tending the flock of his father-in-law, Jethro, he has a vision of a burning bush and hears God call his name. "Moses, Moses," comes the voice. "Come no nearer; take off your sandals, for the place where you are standing is holy ground." And then God identifies himself. "I am the God of your forefathers, the God of Abraham, the God of Isaac, the God of Jacob." And in our day we might add, the God of our foremothers, also—the God of Sarah, the God of Rebecca, the God of Rachel. And we are told that in response Moses covered his face, "for he was afraid to gaze at God" (Ex. 3:4–6). He is then given the commission to lead his people out of bondage, a commission that forms the basis of his life's vocation.

In this dramatic description of heightened spiritual awareness, Moses' vision of God's holiness is quite clear. There is a sense of the numinous which invokes in him feelings of awe and distance. There is an intensely personal quality about the experience leading to a deepened sense of vocation, and there is a sense of set-apartness that applies not only to God but to any thing or any place in which God's holiness is reflected.

Most of the early references to holiness in the Old Testament, like the passage from Exodus, are descriptions of ways of speaking about God and the way in which God is experienced. As this experience becomes more expansive, holiness becomes not only a description of God, but a description of the result of God's impact on creation in general and on human life in particular: "You shall be holy, because I, the Lord your God, am holy." Very early in Israel's history, however, the idea of holiness came to be seen in two rather distinct ways. For the priestly writers, holiness was associated primarily with worship and the sacredness of the Temple in Jerusalem. For those writers associated with the prophetic tradition, holiness was seen more as a description of a people called into covenant with God.

Although these two strands of thought are constantly intermingled throughout biblical history, they are distinct enough to embody two ways of understanding what it means to be holy. In the tradition of the priestly writers we can speak of holy objects and holy places, meaning that because these things are set apart and dedicated to God they partake of God's holiness. This sense of sacred space reaches its highest level in association with the Sabbath, for not only is space hallowed by its relation to God's presence, but so also is time: "God blessed the seventh day and made it holy" (Gen. 2:3).

The priestly idea of the holy has strong overtones in the New Testament. Although there are certainly references in the Old Testament to holiness as a quality in human life (e.g., the people of Israel are often referred to as a "holy people"), it is not until the New Testament that a sense of holiness emerges as an ethical quality related to our personal spiritual quest. Building on an understanding of the nature of holiness derived from the priestly writings—the sense of being set apart and purified by our encounter with the divine—the New Testament writers spoke often of holiness as the fruit of the new life brought about by the life, death, and resurrection of Jesus Christ. Echoing the words of Leviticus, the writer of the first Letter of Peter reminds his fellow Christians, "The One who calls you is holy, like him, be holy in all your behavior, because Scripture says, 'You shall be holy, for I am holy' " (1:16).

It is this idea of holiness, derived largely from the priestly tradition, that has been the dominant emphasis throughout Christian history. Holiness has come to be seen as a particular quality—not clearly defined—that in some way makes one person better than the other. Holiness is often spoken of as something to be achieved, much like the prize at the end of a difficult race. As a result we have tended to limit the designation "holy person" to someone who is really quite out of the ordinary. In doing this I believe we have obscured an image that has much broader application. For holiness is not so much a quality to be acquired as a way of seeing and acting in the day-to-day events of the world.

HOLINESS AS AN IMAGE OF PARTICIPATION

In the prophetic strain of the Old Testament tradition, the idea of the holy is not so much associated with places and things as it is with the people of Israel themselves. In the words of the prophet Micah (6:6–8) Israel had to learn that the holy requires us "to do justly, to love mercy, and to walk humbly before our God." Holiness here is not so much a quality as it is a way of participating in God's vision of human history.

In the New Testament, especially in the Gospel of Luke, this vision of holiness is reflected in Jesus' proclamation of the Kingdom. The prophet Simeon, who had waited in the Temple for the coming of the Messiah, saw in the infant Jesus not just a child who reflected God's presence, but one who in his very person embodied God's vision of the way the world was intended to be. This was the character of Jesus' holiness. "For I have seen with my own eyes," proclaims Simeon, "the deliverance which thou has made ready in full view of all the nations: a light that will be a revelation to the heathen, and glory to thy people Israel" (Luke 2:30–32).

"Holiness in the Bible reaches its climax in Jesus," writes the British theologian Eric James.

He is the holy, fascinating—drawing all people to himself in his love and compassion: yet also the cause of wonder and astonishment, fear and trembling. He was born and died not on days which were holy but on days which were made holy by the way he lived and died on them. He did not live in "the holy land" but in a land that was made holy by the way he spent his day-to-day life there. It was from the raw material of the everyday and ordinary that he fashioned his holiness. And for ever after, for the Christian, wherever we are, whoever we are, whatever the time of day, that moment presents us in our decisions and responsibilities with the raw material out of which the holy has to be fashioned in response to God.[1]

For the Christian, therefore, holiness is the fruit of our association with Jesus. It seems to set us apart, not in the sense of being other-worldly, but rather in the sense of being grasped by the Kingdom vision that formed the center of Jesus' life and message. The call to holiness is a call to live in this world, but not of it— meaning that as we open ourselves to the relationship Jesus offers, we are more and more able to live from a perspective and a vision that transcends what we normally experience.

In the proclamation of Jesus, holiness and the Kingdom of God are indissolubly related. To speak of the Kingdom, however, is not to speak of a goal to be reached, but of a reality that is already present. The moment will come in God's providence when the Kingdom of God will be fulfilled in time—when the blind will see, when the oppressed will be set free, and when all war will cease—but in our present what we experience of these are signs of this new reality. It is like living in a world within another world—one that has different values and different ways of perceiving—just beyond the limits of our sight inviting us to enter. The word holiness, I would like to suggest, describes who we are when that other world impinges on our experience. Despite ourselves, we are different—if only for a moment—from who and what we were before.

JESUS AND THE USE OF PARABLE

One of the most provocative means Jesus used to call people into the Kingdom was to involve them in parables. The parables are a unique story form. They not only involve us in a narrative but, once we are involved and given the eyes to see and the ears to hear (the subject of many of Jesus' parables), they radically alter our perspective about what is true in the world and what is not. Parables are windows into the experience and vision of Jesus. They provide a connection between the world as we know it and the world of the Kingdom, where we are confronted by the unexpected and find our values and perspective suddenly turned upside down.

If the holiness that is offered to us is ever to become a live option for the Church at large, we need to learn again the language of the Kingdom. There is no better place to start than with the parables—learning to hear them not as domesticated folktales, but as the radical challenge to the world's values that they were intended to be.

In an insightful exegesis of the parable of the Good Samaritan, the New Testament scholar Bernard Brandon Scott helps uncover where in this familiar story the radical demand is hidden. The audience at first sees only a man making a journey from Jerusalem to Jericho, a distance of about seventeen miles. The traveler is attacked by robbers and left half-dead in a ditch. As Scott points out, we don't identify with the traveler because of our expectation that helpers will come along. Our tendency, therefore, is not to identify with the victim but with the helpers. And then, one by one, the process of identification is blocked. The priest lets us down, and so does the Levite.

The next character is not the expected Jewish layman, but a Samaritan, the Jews' mortal enemy. Nor does he cooperate with the audience by passing on, but has compassion. The audience now faces a crucial dilemma: identify with the Samaritan or get into the ditch. The first they cannot do; the second is distasteful. Once in the ditch the victim does not consent to the Samaritan's ministrations, he must submit.[2]

For the first-century Jews who were first confronted by this story, the effect was mind-boggling. For a moment they were forced to see the world in a radically new way, and in so doing to experience something of the holiness of God. It is this new way of seeing that is what holiness is about, and why in a profound way it transcends what we often refer to as wholeness. It is concerned with personal growth and self-awareness, but only in a quite specific context. The context is a world where the proud are scattered in their conceit, and where the image of the servant—one person serving another—is the symbol of power.

JESUS AND THE KINGDOM

Modern biblical scholarship has reached almost universal consensus that Jesus' teaching is centered and summed up in his preaching of the Kingdom of God.[3] But because there is no clear description of what the Kingdom is about—no rules for admission—its centrality to the Christian pilgrimage is not always perceived; or if perceived, then it is resisted, because of the radical demand it makes. The Kingdom of God is a vision of what God created the world to be. It is a vision that according to God's plan will ultimately be realized in full, but whose signs are present in the world now, like mustard seed or like leaven. What we have in Jesus' teaching are a number of pictures of the world he sees. When taken individually they seem to stand alone, but when strung together they form the outline of a world in which the values we are used to are reversed. Look for a moment at some of these pictures.

When Jesus inaugurated his ministry, he chose a passage from the prophet Isaiah with which he identified himself (Luke 4:18–21). He came to announce good news to the poor, to proclaim release for prisoners and recovery of sight for the blind, to let the broken victim go free. He identified himself with Zacchaeus the outcast, he broke bread with prostitutes, he reached out to the sinner, and confronted Pontius Pilate in his abuse of power.

When Jesus blessed the peacemakers and the merciful and those who thirsted after righteousness—when he spoke of taking the poor seriously not as a matter of tolerance but as a matter of right—when he called on us to love our enemies and to forgive seventy times seven, he was not offering advice but describing the world in the way he saw it. The vision of the Kingdom Jesus presents to us is a vision of the world seen from the point of view not of the powerful but of the powerless. This, he proclaims, is reality; all else is illusion.

In describing the vision of the Kingdom presented to us in the Gospel of Luke, where this vision is most clearly articulated, Neil Richardson, the British New Testament scholar, offers us a powerful image of what discipleship in the Kingdom—that is, holiness—is about.

Disciples in Luke's eyes are those who have little to rely on to call their own, or, if they have, sit lightly to it ("poor in spirit"). They feel acutely the broken, imperfect nature of human life and of their own in particular, they bear something of the weight of the world's evil with more sorrow than anger, and suffer, for the sake of Christ, the consequences of being often out of step with the power and authorities of their day. Such people might seem to be the flotsam and jetsam of the world, but the teaching which followed shows that, on the contrary, so far from benighted and forlorn, they will find the resources for loving to a quite remarkable extent, and find themselves in the possession of the peace, inner freedom and wealth which comes from God.[4]

You can understand when you read a description like this why we have so much resistance to the Kingdom vision. You can understand also why Luke, in describing entrance into the Kingdom, uses such images as a narrow door or the eye of a needle. There is no way to enter the Kingdom without some perceptual change. The Gospel Jesus preaches is one of eschatological reversal. The time will come when those on the edge of society will come to the center, a time when conditions between rich and poor, the powerful and the powerless, will be reversed. This is what the images of the Kingdom suggest—not a plan for revolution or an ideal society, but an invitation to rich and poor alike to see with an inner vision. This is not Marxism or liberal fantasy, but the very center of Jesus' teaching. As Thomas Hoyt observes, "For Luke, the Kingdom belongs to the poor, but the rich share in it by virtue of their treatment of the poor and needy."[5] This is the demand that the Gospel places upon us: Not that we go out and sell all our possessions, but that we begin to perceive the world as it is viewed by those most on the edge; or, if only for a moment, to walk in the shoes of those whom normally we do not see; or to feel in our bones the passion that motivated the prophets. If the Kingdom were only demand, it would be a burden beyond our bearing. But the Kingdom as Jesus proclaims it is offered as a gift—the fruit of a deepening relationship in him.

Neil Richardson has written: "Jesus taught that God was not only more demanding than people cared to think, but also more generous than they dared to hope."[6] We are asked nothing by God that he does not empower us to do. He empowers us to love, for we are called not to walk alone, but in Christ, whose holiness we share. From the point of view of modern geopolitics, the Christian vision is utopian. But until this vision of the Kingdom is incarnated in the human spirit, there can be no context in which the human family can live together without destroying itself. To speak of the thirst for holiness, then, is to speak of a moral vision and a capacity for love that comes from the source of creation itself. Holiness is that which expands our humanity, for it not only provides the context in which growth takes place, but provides a vision of what life is ultimately about and towards which we stumble and slowly make our way, owning our brokenness but rejoicing in the Grace that alone will make us whole. "O Worship the Lord in the beauty of holiness," cries the Psalmist, "let the whole earth stand in awe of him. For he cometh, for he cometh to judge the earth, and with righteousness to judge the world and the peoples with his truth (Ps. 96:9, 13).

The Holy Person in
Contemporary Society

3.

In the Fall of 1984 it was the good fortune of the General Theological Seminary in New York City to have in its midst the Right Reverend Desmond Tutu of South Africa, who during this time was awarded the Nobel Prize for Peace. The impact of this event on the seminary community was an unequaled personal as well as educational experience. For everyone who was then a part of the seminary community was confronted with an experience of the holy in moments of both high drama and profound simplicity.

Desmond Tutu is a short and wiry man with energy that is boundless. He has a capacity to engage people with such single-minded attention that, even when surrounded by crowds, the one spoken to is made to feel that he or she is indeed personally addressed. His sense of humor, his personal warmth, and his quick intelligence are empowering, and to be with him is to feel oneself enhanced. He is a man whose life has been deeply touched by the Holy Spirit and who sustains this with an easy but highly disciplined life of prayer. His passion for humanity is shown in the eloquence of his cry for justice, which seems to lie behind every word he speaks.

After listening to the bishop address a seminary gathering, a student turned to me and said unhesitatingly, "Today, I have met a holy man." A little later I asked him to elaborate a bit on what he had meant. I found his response to be extremely helpful. "What I experienced in Bishop Tutu's presence," the student said, "enabled me to experience the Christ in my own life. It was as if I was drawn into my own center by some magnetic force. But at the same time, I found that the world seemed different. The cry of human pain suddenly became less peripheral to my vision, and what had before seemed blurred and distant suddenly became focused. But the remarkable thing was that all this seemed to occur in the

midst of quite ordinary events. It was not so much that Bishop
Tutu was so special, but that he communicated something beyond
himself that could be honestly experienced."

I have thought about these words many times since, words that
in different ways have been confirmed by my own experience.
Christianity, as many have pointed out, is not concerned primarily
with religion, but with the way people see and embrace life. Although Desmond Tutu is a bishop in the Anglican Church of
South Africa on whom God has bestowed many special gifts,
there is nothing about the holiness he reflects that is not equally
available to all whose lives are strongly influenced by the Spirit of
God. In baptism, Christians believe, our lives are united with the
Risen Christ in such a way that it is possible in any given moment
for us to reflect his holiness. When the student who met Bishop
Tutu spoke of experiencing the holiness of God, he was describing
what it is like to feel oneself empowered by both new energy and
new vision. He was made freshly aware of God's presence already
within him, and at the same time he was enabled to see the world
from a Kingdom perspective: People who were normally seen on
the margins of life became more visible, and he felt an intensifica-
tion of a sense of God's righteousness and compassion. He experienced these things through Bishop Tutu because Bishop Tutu was
experiencing them himself, and I in turn experienced the same
sense of holiness through the student with whom I was talking.

The call to be a holy person is fundamental to what is implied in
our baptism. It involves the premise that if we are grounded in the
person of Christ, we will experience his holiness in the most ordinary events of our lives. Not only will our lives be deepened as a
result, but we will be instruments of the holiness of God to others.
The experience of holiness takes us beyond what we normally
mean when we speak of a "good Christian." For holiness is not
limited to those whose lives are primarily church-centered, but extends to those whose energies are expended in dealing with the
complexities of the world. Holiness is only tangentially related to
how active we are in the institutional church—how many com-
mittees we serve on, how many conferences we attend, how fa-

miliar we are with religious language. Holiness is a description of what happens when the experience of God that is deepened in us in the life of the gathered Church drives us into the events of day-to-day life with a new perspective and new energy for all that the Kingdom of God seeks to convey. Holiness is not so much concerned about "being religious" as it is with perspective and values and openness to the Spirit of God present in the world. Holiness is not a status we achieve, but the energy and vision we are given as a result of our encounter with the holiness of God in the midst of the complexities of human experience.

A LOOK AHEAD

The religious historian and social commentator Martin Marty was recently invited to contribute to a time capsule that was to be placed in the foundation stone of the River City complex in Chicago. The capsule, slated to be opened in the year 2000, contains reflections on the present by many luminaries in a variety of fields of interest. Marty's reflections are extremely provocative:

In 1984, the strongest spiritual (or anti-spiritual) force internationally was tribalism. Tribalism calls me to link "my" gods-people-place-culture over against "their" gods-people-place-culture in an endless cycle of defensive and aggressive acts. During the next 15 years, tribalism will increase among peoples in the Asian subcontinent, the Middle East, much of Africa, and in milder forms, in America. In an age of terrorism and easily available weaponry, it will remain a destructive force. As the old secular synthesis which has promoted faith in progress, reason, science, and tolerance was tested, if not shattered, many American intellectuals turned tribalist themselves.

Nowhere in the world during these years of "the short pull" will major or mass groups that promote empathy, tolerance and responsiveness between people and groups prosper as will introverted and aggressive groups. At the very end of this period, nothing having been gained and much having been lost, some people with a "long pull" vision will be seen to have endured. The American polity, "the Republic," will have somehow survived and will remain a frail instrument for more positive intergroup relations. Some new faith in human interaction, real "ecumenical" ideals, will find advocates. Meanwhile, religion itself will have been put to work also more positively to sustain personal life in tense times, to promote meaning in life, to enable individuals and small groups to encourage the acts of love, to contribute to health and well-being, to provide solace for the many, hope for most and courage for the few.[1]

WORLDLY HOLINESS AND HOLY WORLDLINESS

The biblical vision of holiness is never something that is disengaged from life. We can speak therefore of worldly holiness when we see in someone those qualities referred to by Dr. Marty—frail instruments able to remain faithful to a vision of human solidarity even in the midst of violence, people able to promote meaning in life in the midst of confusion, and people able to empower others with solace, courage, and hope. These are not simple tasks, nor are they tasks that can be accomplished apart from a personal sense of relatedness to the redemptive energy of God in the world. Wholeness in God's eyes mirrors human solidarity on a global scale. As Margaret Dewey has written, "Christ in the life of the world means to know differently. It also means to live differently."[2] It is in these areas of difference between what God has called the world to be and what we as sinful human beings have made it that holiness can be seen and experienced.

We can speak of holy worldliness when referring to those people whose activity in the world has a way of making something we normally think of as secular seem sacred. When Lewis Thomas writes of the life of a cell, or when we read of the heroic efforts of a surgeon to save one human life, we encounter the reality of the sacred. "To teach, heal, engineer, defend at the bar, or make beautiful things in a spirit of justice and helpfulness is to bend work toward the service of Christ's kingdom," writes the educator John Carmody. "To feed, clothe, repair or counsel as though people were members of one another, radical equals, is to baptize work and make it whole."[3]

Holiness in everyday life is directly related to worship. Here the mundane is offered to God to be consecrated and given back for our use again. Holiness is the fruit of worship, for worship takes us out of ourselves and places our lives in perspective. It opens us to the holy, for it allows us to experience and recognize those special moments when the sacred and secular are made one.

In "A Father's Story," a beautiful story by André Dubus, a very down-to-earth Luke Ripley apologizes for his lack of interest or ability in the art of meditation, which he hears so many people speak about, and tells what it means for him as a very secular man to participate week after week in the celebration of the Eucharist in his local church. He does not pretend that "going to church" is necessarily an experience of great fulfillment, but he notes what the habit of familiar patterns means to him. "Ritual," he muses, "allows those who cannot will themselves out of the secular to perform the spiritual, as dancing allows the tongue-tied man a ceremony of love."[4]

In a description such as this, I find the holiness of God revealed. Not in a special act of superhuman or super-religious piety, but as the fruit of a kind of faithfulness that draws us into this world with an increasing sense of who we are in Christ and who it is he calls us to be. Holiness, when viewed this way, is not an achievement, but the gift of our personhood offered to God in faith and received back again consecrated by his holiness and infused with his life.

LIVING A HOLY LIFE

The call to a holy life is extended to everyone whose life has been touched by the reality of God. Holiness is not the fruit of specialness, but of faithfulness. For to be faithful in a relationship is to honor it by the way we live. The call to holiness in our day, as it has always been, is a call to live in the world as a sign of the Kingdom. It is a call to participate in those things that contribute to human solidarity, forgiveness and compassion, righteousness and justice, and ultimately, global peace (shalom!).

Holiness, because it is the fruit of our relationship with Jesus Christ, is something that the simplest person can (and often does) reflect; but because God uses the whole world to carry out his plan of redemption, holiness can be manifested in all people of faith. There are, however, certain qualities that seem to heighten the experience of holiness in our time.

First of all, when we experience holiness in another person, or become bearers of the holy ourselves, a particular kind of connection seems to occur. To describe this connection, we use such phrases as "a sense of presence," or "an awareness of single-minded attention," or of "the Christ in another and Christ in ourselves being experienced as one"—something like what Martin Buber described as the experience of "I-Thou." It is that deep care for people which is always an expression of holiness—a caring for people that is neither condescending nor patronizing, but which frees us to respond to what God in the depth of our being calls us to be. When the student at the General Theological Seminary referred to Desmond Tutu's capacity for single-minded attention, he was describing this phenomenon. It is a phenomenon, however, which is not limited to religious heroes, but is manifest in ordinary people who have opened the deep place of their hearts to the working of the Spirit.

A second characteristic of holiness in our time describes the capacity to create neutral space where people can hold ideas or opinions without having to defend them to the death. Some people have a way of creating healing space even in the midst of what seems unresolvable conflict. Often these people have little consciousness of what they are doing. They are, in a very real sense, instruments of peace. By their very presence a change of mood—a shift in the emotional environment—allows healing to take place. Whenever this happens we know we have encountered the holy. Although we can't produce this automatically, we can develop skills that help create the conditions where holy space can emerge.

Nothing is more critical for human survival than fulfilling a need as simple (and yet as difficult) as this. The only way we can break through tribal barriers is to provide space—intellectual, emotional, and geographic—where exploration can take place. A church or an individual Christian whose center is deeply rooted in

Christ can be far more effective opening doors than making pronouncements. There are obviously times when Christians need to speak out with forcefulness and conviction, and we need the courage and wisdom to do this more often than we do. However, given the diversity of voices that claim to speak in the name of Christ, what we say must be part of a larger strategy that has some clear outcome in mind. Passion that lacks the homework that goes into planning what's next all too often sounds like the preacher who shouts the loudest when he has the least to say.

To know this, of course, is to realize how very important it is to deal with the world as it really is. We cannot speak of the Church without acknowledging its complicity in most of the problems that the world faces. Holiness is not a euphemism for moral blindness or ecclesiastical imperialism. Holiness emerges out of the recognition that we are all sinners in the sight of God and moves on from there. Holiness by its very nature demands that we view reality as honestly as we can, including honesty about ourselves. For much of the Church's witness is diminished not only by a failure to do the homework necessary to get our facts straight, but by a basic lack of humility that distorts what we see. Holiness as a quality is the fruit of a perspective that begins with the words, "God, have mercy upon me, a sinner!"

Third, holiness in human life always embodies the Kingdom vision. When we encounter holiness in another person, we are, as has been noted before, helped to see differently. We become bearers of the holy to others when this vision is so incarnated in our own lives that people see through us. The task of the Christian Church in the world is to call people to that vision of what God intends for the world—not as a club to coerce, but as a message to inspire hope. To do this, we must grasp this vision for ourselves and wrestle with its day-to-day pragmatic implications. It does no good to talk about world peace unless we can offer one step that can be taken to get us beyond where we are now. If the larger vision is real to us, we can afford to be less dogmatic about the various pieces that make it up. For as Paul reminds us, we *do* see through a dark glass where our perception of the whole is but partial.

The call to holiness ultimately leads us to that point where we must make hard choices, those which own the awful anxiety of ambiguity without taking the easy way out. Hard choices always leave room for exceptions without fear of sacrificing the essential truth that needs to be preserved. Holiness demands, however, that we never stand behind a principle until we have experienced what is at stake for the people most affected—and this involves issues as emotion-laden as homosexuality or abortion or racial justice, as well as issues that seem more distant. The hard choice is to choose, knowing that in another situation we might have to choose differently—where we must choose the best of a number of bad solutions. Our choice, however, comes not in an effort to relieve the anxiety that is inside us, but to move in a direction that in the long view affirms those values inherent in Jesus' proclamation of the Kingdom of God, values where people take precedence over abstract principle.

THE HOLY IN OUR MIDST

The holiness of God is all around us, but it is not something easily recognized. Although the experience of the holy is direct (we know we have encountered something out of the ordinary), it is reflected in people whose lives are as complex as our own. In Mother Teresa of Calcutta, the world experienced a vision of holiness; but as soon as she came to the world's attention, she was criticized for her failure to challenge the system that produced the conditions of poverty and hunger to which she was responding. The criticism, I suspect, was accurate; but rather than diminishing the holiness Mother Teresa reflected, it simply reminded us of her humanity. Holiness and perfection are not synonyms.

If Martin Marty is right in his analysis of the world that is emerging, the place to look for holiness will be in those areas where conflict is the most acute—where God somehow manages to raise up "frail instruments" able to remain faithful to a vision of human solidarity even in the midst of violence, people able to promote meaning in life in the midst of confusion, and people able to empower others with strength, courage, and hope. Many areas come immediately to mind—places where conflict has erupted in terrorism and violence. Already we have seen holy people emerge in Lebanon, Northern Ireland, Central America, and South Africa, offering to the world a vision of what might be, and sometimes making their offering at tremendous personal cost, including death.

But there are other less obvious areas of conflict in which we need to look for holiness. In the debates, charges, and counter-charges that have already been stimulated by the Roman Catholic Bishops' pastoral on the economy, the holy will most certainly emerge. When we speak about how a society organizes its resources, whom it is responsive to, and what its vision is, we are talking about a Kingdom vision. As the gap between rich and poor becomes wider, we are being prepared for a radical shift in consciousness that will make it possible for us to see what most of us cannot see now. This will occur, I believe, as the holy emerges in ways we least expect.

Another area of conflict in our time is pushing the world toward deeper polarization, a polarization that will no doubt harden before new possibilities will emerge. The role and contribution of women in human society is not just an issue that is confronting Western society. It is an issue of exploding consequences in Islamic and many Third World societies. Because our understanding of sexuality—of what it means to be male and female—is fundamental to our understanding of humanity, it draws us to the very core of God's vision of creation. The conflicts we experience over abortion, homosexuality, and gender are deeply divisive, causing hurt and crippling injury in more ways than we can imagine. The holiness we look for will not be seen in who can shout the loudest, or make the most coercive claim for the principles they will defend to the death; but rather, holiness will appear in those people who can take us beyond where we are now and allow us to see in them something new. The holy might appear in people we least expect. Indeed, the holy might emerge in us.

The invitation to holiness in our time is serious business. It is an invitation presented to each of us in the many settings in which we find ourselves—in the workplace, in the political realm, in our communities and families and churches. It is an invitation to be used in a particular way for the opening stage of a new vision about what God intends for the world and to become in our own lives instruments of healing and grace.

INVITATION TO HOLINESS

In the midst of the daily struggle of ordinary people to find meaning and hope in their lives, God is present, seeking to reveal himself (or herself, as we are being challenged to consider). God's holiness is everywhere—enlightening the dark places of our lives and the institutions in which we live and work. We cannot limit the healing power of God only to those areas where we are comfortable. The call to share in the ministry of Jesus Christ is a call to embrace the world in both its pain and possibility, knowing that it is in the embrace itself that the holiness of God will be revealed and our next step made more clear. Herein "lies the richness of God's free grace lavished upon us, imparting full wisdom and insight. He has made known to us his hidden purpose—such was his will and pleasure determined beforehand in Christ—to put into effect when the time was ripe: namely, that the universe, all in heaven and on earth, might be brought into a unity in Christ" (Eph. 1:8–10). It is in words such as these that God's call to holiness is offered to us all.

Pastoral Dimensions
of Holiness

4.

"Holiness," as one sensitive observer has described it, "is not some object which is finally possessed, as in personal property; or some place which is finally reached; rather, it is a relationship which God establishes and develops. Holiness is not having something; it is being something."[1] The task of the church, therefore, is not to produce holiness, as if this were even possible, but rather to cultivate an environment in which the thirst for holiness is experienced and seen as something fundamental to our humanity. It is the cultivation of this environment which I understand to be the primary task of the church's ministry today—an environment that includes the inner lives of each of us as well as the communal life of the church itself.

In the formation of the pastoral ministry of the Christian Church—in which I include all the ways in which we contribute to human nurture and growth—three distinct strands began to emerge early in the Church's history. As described today they involve pastoral care, moral guidance, and spiritual direction. As best one can tell, pastoral care emerged in the New Testament Church as the expression of concern for the care and relief of widows and others in need. Moral guidance developed in response to the need, accentuated by the persecution and harassment of the first century, to provide help for people seeking to live the ethical lives demanded by the community of faith. Education was education in discipleship shaped by a strong moral imperative. Spiritual direction emerged as a distinct concern of the Church in an effort to help people develop and maintain the inner discipline necessary for ongoing life in Christ. With the rampant secular accommodation that occurred during the Constantinian period (third and fourth centuries), spiritual guidance was given particular visibility as Christians began flocking to the desert to seek guidance from those who had withdrawn from the world in a solitary life of prayer. However expressed—and I'm sure that the ways were as varied as they are today—pastoral ministry in the life of the Church, very early in our history, was composed of three distinct but closely interconnected strands: the care and nurture of persons in need, moral guidance and education, and spiritual direction.

SEPARATE BUT NOT EQUAL

The renewal of pastoral theology in the life of the Church (or practical theology, as the discipline is now being called) is directly related to the recovery of these three strands that have historically shaped the Church's response to human need. The psychological revolution of the late nineteenth and early twentieth centuries not only opened up the human unconscious as a field for exploration, but provided new methodologies and even a new language, which ultimately rent the field of pastoral care asunder. Pastoral care became a sophisticated and separate discipline, certainly wiser and more humane than before, but often disconnected from its theological roots. Moral guidance in many instances lapsed into a rather joyless moralism (or casuistry, depending on the tradition from which it came), or else was secularized and taken over by public education. Spiritual direction seems to have been either abandoned altogether in reaction to what seemed to be an over-emphasis on justification by work, or was otherwise allowed to rigidify in the backwaters of pre-Vatican II Roman Catholic thought. From time to time great figures have emerged to challenge this separation, but for the Church at large, these voices have been hard to hear.

All these stirrings and realignments, of course, were the culmination of a long process of secularization that began with the Enlightenment. Secular agencies emerged to provide care and services. Educational institutions and governments were looked to for guidance on how we should live, as the Church's role became less clearly defined. For some time, the Christian Church has struggled to find where in fact its unique contribution lies. The introduction of modern psychological thought helped temporarily to resolve this crisis—giving the Church something to grab hold of—and so pastoral care came to be associated with psychological and therapeutic help. We are beginning to emerge now into a new era of understanding—an era when the theological dimension has become more prominent, not in the sense of diminishing the insights of the secular sciences, but rather in the sense of infusing them with new meaning.

The care of people in need, the concern for embracing the moral vision the Kingdom embodies, and training in the life of prayer are not separate entities. They are three strands of a whole, necessary for a full response to the call of holiness.

In the Church today each of these strands constitutes a discipline in itself with a body of knowledge drawn from both secular and theological tradition. My concern here, however, is not to explore or critique these particular disciplines per se, but rather to suggest a primary image in each strand that might help to offer a corrective to the way each of these strands is normally expressed in the life of the Church. The images I want to lift up are contained in three common biblical words: compassion, righteousness, and companionship. Each of these reflects the holiness given to us as the fruit of participation with Christ in the Kingdom, whenever and wherever this occurs.

COMPASSION AND THE CARE OF PEOPLE IN NEED

The primary aim of pastoral care in the life of the Church is to provide nurture and support for the Christian community in its individual and communal quest for wholeness. It is in the context of this quest that holiness emerges, the test of which is in the deepening of the gift of compassion. Wholeness without compassion is of little value, for compassion is in itself an expression of holiness.

The impact of the life of Jesus Christ on the world is the result not of his achievement, but of his compassion, which reaches its climax in his self-offering on the Cross on behalf of the world, including those persons who were responsible for his death. According to even the most minimal standards of success, Jesus achieved very little in his ministry; but in the hearts and minds of those he touched, his compassion made it possible for help to be experienced in a new way.

Compassion means literally "to suffer with." It is love empowered by holiness. It is a gift that moves us beyond ourselves to a point where we are able to identify with the pain and brokenness of others. Compassion necessitates a connection in which we both give and receive. It is the gift that lies at the heart of our humanity. Without it, we very rapidly become hard and brittle. With it, we become bearers of the holy to others. Wherever Jesus went, he displayed an innate sensitivity to those in need. He overcame the self-deprecation of Zacchaeus by giving him a new sense of himself. He gave Mary Magdalene a sense of worth, and he gave the beggar hope. He was an advocate for those who were powerless, and a source of strength with those struggling with what often seemed to be the sheer incomprehensibility of life.

"Compassion," wrote the authors of a book by that name, "asks us to go where it hurts, to enter into places of pain, to share in weakness, fear, confusion, and anguish." They continue,

Compassion challenges us to cry out with those in misery, to move in with those who are lonely, to weep with those in tears. Compassion requires us to be weak with the weak, vulnerable with those who are vulnerable. When we look at compassion this way, it becomes clear that something more is intended than a general kindness or tender-heartedness. It is not surprising that compassion, understood as suffering with, often invokes in us a deep resistance or even protest. It is important for us to acknowledge this resistance and recognize that suffering is not something we desire or to which we are attracted. And yet, it is our compassion, received as a gift, and haltingly expressed, that leads us to the heart of Christ.[2]

I acknowledge the resistance to which the authors of this very powerful testimony refer. I have difficulty being a compassionate person because I have difficulty being compassionate with myself. When I am in conflict over all the things I think I *ought* to do (and the need is beyond reckoning), I find that I end up doing nothing. None of our motives are pure. Sin and self-interest mar the most noble act. To be compassionate, therefore, begins with the ability (often discovered only after hard struggle) to be forgiving of ourselves as we try to focus our life and deepen its quality. We cannot respond to every need. Some needs we are not equipped to respond to, others we are. Compassion involves knowing the difference.

We become compassionate people by acting compassionately. For most of us this means embracing new experiences and unfamiliar situations. It means accepting the risk of being gently pushed to move beyond what is naturally comfortable—beyond our edges, if you will, trusting that in so doing we will encounter in new and surprising ways the holiness of God.

In *The White Hotel*, the British novelist D. M. Thomas combines fact with fantasy in a compelling way to give us a fresh vision of the Kingdom. Lisa, the principal figure in the novel, becomes involved in the Holocaust. Because she is only half-Jewish, she could have denied her identity; but she chooses, for a number of reasons, to identify with the Jews in their suffering—a choice that results in her own agonizing death. Suddenly the novel slips from the present into a future time—a time beyond death—when the characters in the novel meet again, but not as one might expect. The vision of the Kingdom is not presented as a time when all is healed, but rather as a time when there is the opportunity to heal.

Many thousands of immigrants were waiting, standing by their packed wooden suitcases and holding their bundles of rags tied with string. They look, not sad—listless; not thin—skeletal; not angry—patient. Lisa sighed. "Why is it like this, Richard? We were made to be happy and to enjoy life. What's happened?" He shook his head in bafflement, and breathed out smoke. "We were made to be happy? You're an incurable optimist, old girl." He stubbed his cigarette, and took the baton from his belt. "We're desperately short of nurses," he says. "Can you help?" He pointed his baton toward the casualty unit. Camp beds had spilled out onto the grounds. White figures were scurrying among them. "Yes, of course," she said. She hurried toward the unit, breaking into a run.[3]

And as she runs to involve herself in the chaos that surrounds her, she discovers that the pain of her wounds has disappeared and in some mysterious way she begins to experience a flood of joy.

Holiness is the fruit of compassion. It is born on our response to those sometimes sudden invitations presented by God to share in the compassion of Christ. The questions these invitations present to us, however, is the question posed by Thomas's novel: *What is the meaning of human life*—indeed, of our lives? Does the meaning of life involve the pursuit of happiness as we have always known it, or is happiness the fruit of a different understanding of reality, which most of us have only glimpsed—a reality where compassion stands not on the periphery of life but at its center? This is a question of desperate importance that ultimately each of us must answer for ourselves.

MORAL SENSITIVITY AND THE THIRST FOR RIGHTEOUSNESS

No doubt because of a natural and much needed reaction to the moralism of earlier days, the idea of "thirsting for righteousness" has not been a particularly strong element in most of the education that goes on in the Church today. Either the moral dimension of life is presented largely in terms of "ought," or else in such relative and noncontroversial ways that it loses its power to shape human consciousness.

The biblical use of the word "righteousness" is the moral equivalent of what we mean when we speak of holiness. It incorporates such concerns as a passion for justice and a concern for truth along with the need to live an ethically responsible life. It involves reflecting in what we *do* the Christian moral vision by which we understand who we *are*. Righteousness is the human expression of holiness embodying a vision rooted in moral perspective. In the New Testament the same word is used for righteousness that is used for justification. As New Testament scholar John Koenig puts it, righteousness is God making things right.

It is impossible to understand the person of Jesus without coming to terms with his relationship to the law of Moses. Jesus was a child of the Law. He embodied it in his very person. He was able to fulfill the Law because he was obedient to it. The power of Jesus' message emerged from the holiness of his life, and the holiness he embodied was rooted in that moral vision present in those ancient commandments given to Moses at Sinai and expounded by the prophets. The significance of this, I must confess, is a relatively new insight for me, despite thirty years in the ordained ministry. I was brought up very much a child of Grace—or so I thought—in strong reaction to any suggestion that salvation could be earned. I have come to see the degree to which I have used this truth to support what in reality has been a flight from the Law. The Law for me has been primarily a parent from which I sought to be free. In growing up in the Christian faith, the sense of the holiness and wonder of the Law simply was not present.

Holiness, I believe, involves rediscovering the moral vision Jesus embodies in a way that invokes in us a sense of thirst rather than demand. "Happy are they who have not walked in the counsel of the wicked, nor lingered in the way of sinners, nor sat in the seat of the scornful! Their *delight* is in the law of the Lord, and they meditate on his law day and night" (Ps. 1:1–2). "O Lord I *love* your Law; all the day long it is on my mind" (Ps. 119:97). The commandments of God have too often been presented in our tradition only as moral precepts by which we can judge our neighbors, rather than as a vision in which the call to holiness is rooted. Our concern is not to have presented to us a blueprint for life that will allow us to avoid risk, but rather a vision of integrity from which decisions are made and life is lived. Similarly, our concern for the Law and the prophetic insight into the power of evil as it operates in the world is not to win God's acceptance by so-called right behavior, but to know within ourselves the desperate need we have for the Grace offered to us in Jesus Christ.

In John Braine's *Room at the Top*, Joe Lampton returns to his friends after receiving the news that his girlfriend has been killed in an automobile accident, a tragedy for which Joe feels very much responsible. As he enters the room where his friends are gathered, the response is immediate, "Nobody blames you, Joe. Nobody blames you." But there is a long silence as he ponders what they are saying. Finally he speaks. "O my God," he says, "that's precisely the trouble."[4]

"I am the Lord thy God, thou shalt have no other gods but me." "Thou shalt not steal." "Thou shalt not commit adultery." And as the Scripture unfolds, the call for righteousness broadens. "Hear, you heads of Jacob, and rulers of the house of Israel! Is it not for you to know justice? You who have the good and love the evil." "What does the Lord require, to do justice, to love mercy, to walk humbly with our God" (Mic. 3:2; 6:8). These are not casual words unrelated to human growth. They embody a vision that helps us to define who we are and what in Christ we are called to be.

Don Browning, in *The Moral Context of Pastoral Care*, speaks of the need of the church to become "a community of moral inquiry."[5] This suggests an environment where the issues that confront us, often leaving us paralyzed, are seen as formative issues for Christian nurture and must therefore be addressed as issues not on the edges of the church's life but at its very center. Moral guidance and support must begin with the youngest child and continue with the oldest adult. It means standing with our friends as they wrestle with the difficult moral decision presented by the marketplace; it means being politically sensitive and alert to the moral dimension of the way in which nations and groups deal with each other, particularly in respect to the use of power; but moral guidance also means being aware of how the conscience is formed and how we develop as moral persons. Lawrence Kohlberg, in his discussion of the stages of moral development, speaks of the passion for justice as the sign of moral maturity; and Carol Gilligan, in a fascinating analysis of the difference in moral development between women and men, speaks of "principled non-violence" as the sign of moral maturity. In commenting on these theories of moral development, however, Gabriel Moran offers another perspective.

We cannot attain a virtuous character by aggressively acquiring the virtues, one after another. Character results from how we respond with a self that has been given to each of us, to the social setting and physical environment in which we live. Morality is unavoidably response, but the question, is response to what?[6]

The answer lies in our vision of the Kingdom and the righteousness it embodies. The lure of holiness calls us to grow as moral beings. It, by the Grace of God, initiates in us a thirst for righteousness; but it is a thirst that needs constant tending, gentle guidance, and an acceptance of frailty in ourselves and others. Righteousness is not a club, or a cause, but a response to a vision of the world as it was created to be. It is in itself a sip of holiness.

COMPANIONSHIP, SPIRITUAL DIRECTION, AND OUR EXPERIENCE OF HOLINESS

In the Gospel of Luke we are told that the disciples were sent out on their first journey in the Lord two by two (10:1). It was in companionship that their journey began, and it was in companionship that it continued. Companionship in Christ involves not only mutual support, but a relationship in which we can become "soul friends" to one another. In a formal sense such a relationship has been formally referred to as spiritual direction or spiritual guidance, but as this is lived out it involves one Christian helping another in their journey in Christ. Companionship, because it reflects something fundamental about relationships in the Kingdom, is a sign of holiness.

I find helpful the distinctions made between pastoral counseling, psychotherapy, and spiritual direction by Gerald May, the distinguished psychiatrist and interpreter of the spiritual life. Despite overlaps, he insists, there are fundamental and critical differences between these disciplines in content, process, and objective. Psychotherapy, he suggests, is interested primarily in self-understanding, pastoral counseling in self-determination, and spiritual direction in self-surrender to the discerned will of God.

I would expand these definitions a bit to suggest that psychotherapy works primarily (but certainly not exclusively) with unconscious material, relying heavily on the principle of transference. Pastoral counseling, on the other hand, focuses primarily on conscious material, problem solving, and support, paying particular attention to issues of faith and vocation. Spiritual direction is concerned almost exclusively with our relationship to God and the way in which this relationship is manifested in both the interior and exterior aspects of our lives.

Spiritual direction, then, more than any other discipline, is concerned with the way we experience the holiness of God, and the impact this makes on our lives. Spiritual direction or spiritual guidance—or maybe better still, spiritual friendship—involves one person helping another to be more receptive to the movement of the Spirit in the way they pray and in the way they act. Although many spiritual direction relationships are highly disciplined and quite structured, the vast majority are informal and represent a common exploration into what the call to holiness is about.

Although in some sense all Christians could be said to be on a spiritual pilgrimage, for most people the journey is vague and unarticulated. And even if acknowledged, the church is often not seen as a primary source of help. To speak of spiritual direction in parish life, therefore, is to speak in the broadest possible terms. Whenever we assist people to reflect seriously on the quality and direction of their lives we are engaged in spiritual direction. Our aim is to assist one another in our movement into holiness, beginning where we are and helping to discern where God wants us to be. It involves listening in the spirit of prayer. It involves asking questions that enable people to reflect more deeply on their understanding of God ("When you think of God, how would you describe what comes to mind?"). It involves helping people develop disciplines of prayer that are not forced, but conform to the kind of people they are and the demands life makes upon them. Spiritual direction is concerned with helping people see the world through the eyes of Christ ("Where in what you have to tell me do you experience yourself being challenged by the Kingdom, and how are you going to respond?").

Kenneth Leech, in *The Social God*, argues for the revival of spiritual direction that is "non-clerical, which is not problem centered, but which is rooted in the common life of the Body of Christ. This must involve emphasis on prophecy, vision, and spirituality in action."[7] To give substance to what is an extremely important contribution to our understanding of the relation of spiritual direction to the pursuit of holiness, Leech in another context spells out what he calls his "Seven Theses for Spiritual Direction and Social Justice." Because Leech's work has been so helpful to me in my own thinking, I would like to quote these theses in full:

1. Spiritual direction involves finding a theological direction, an orientation, which will build up the movement of the Kingdom of God.
2. The quest for social justice is inseparable from the quest for personal holiness and personal reward.
3. There is a clear trend towards a spirituality of self-cultivation which cuts at the root of social commitment.
4. Spiritual direction is discipline for pioneers, not settlers.
5. The locus for spiritual direction should normally be the parish or local Christian community, not the specialized institute, the clinic, the counselling center or the academy.
6. The renewal of contemplative prayer and the re-awakening of vision is the necessary preliminary to any renewal of prophecy.
7. As the position of Christians in Western Society becomes more precarious, there will be a growing need for nourishment and group support.[8]

The task of the parish, if it is to help create a climate where holiness is experienced, could well begin by enabling those already experienced in prayer to enable others. There are throughout the country several programs in spiritual direction (including one now well-established at the General Theological Seminary in New York, where I serve). These programs provide training to clergy and laity who will in turn help others. A good place to begin in raising the consciousness of a congregation might well be Leech's seven theses.

It is hard to describe to someone else what it is like to experience the presence of God. It can happen in a very secular context—looking at a painting or walking along a city street, in the incredible mystery of prayer, or in a relationship with another person. There is a sense of power, sometimes accompanied by a flash of emotion, and then the sparkle of a new insight or a new measure of self-understanding. For the people who create space in their lives for this kind of awareness to develop and deepen, the sense of God's presence becomes for them an increasingly transforming experience. In the silence of prayer, lives are changed. Sometimes a conflict is resolved deep within us, or the anxiety that has blocked us for so long seems suddenly to melt away. But more often than not, the experience of God's presence brings with it new vision and new strength to use our lives in a different way. Contemplative living—and, of course, this is what the life of prayer really is about—is more than anything else a matter of learning to see.

THE PARISH CHURCH AND THE THREE-FOLD STRAND

Pastoral care is essential for the building and sustaining of Christian community. It is also an essential component in the task we share with others of keeping the religious impulse alive under the pressures of modern life. I am arguing for the return of pastoral care to its roots—roots that involve a response to the moral dimensions of the Kingdom in our midst, ministries of caring that involve the whole people of God, and the restoration of spiritual guidance and companionship as something normative in parish life. The recovery of such an emphasis will mean for most churches a significant reordering of priorities. It will mean taking seriously the theological roots of what it means for one human being to care for another so that we can more fully understand and appreciate the very special and critical contribution the Christian Church has to make toward the healing of the world's pain.

We are speaking of a recovery in the normative life of the parish church, and in the everyday life of the average Christian, of a vision of holiness that in itself has transforming power. In it is this same vision of holiness we see incarnated in the person of Jesus, and which, incredible as it may seem, is available to us. What Jesus is, he gives without measure. Behold! "When anyone is united to Christ, there is a new world; the old order has gone, and a new order has begun . . . and he has enlisted us in this service of reconciliation" (2 Cor. 5:17, 19).

Prayer and the
Kingdom Vision

5.

In the proclamation of Jesus, holiness and the Kingdom of God are indissolubly related. To live in Christ is to live a life tuned to the new reality which through the Spirit is continuously impinging on our consciousness. The question to which we now turn is about what we must do to be open to the possibility of holiness as it is presented to us.

The gift of holiness—which, as has been suggested earlier, is in reality the gift of our full humanity—is received when we are able to see the world in a new way, when in faith we are able to discern and respond to God's vision of the world through the eyes of Christ. This kind of seeing is the fruit of a contemplative vision—a vision that can only be nourished in solitude and in prayer. Prayer for the Christian therefore is not something added to our lives, something extra we do, but rather it is as fundamental to our lives as the act of breathing. It is through prayer that we are caught up in the rhythm and the energy of the Kingdom that is amongst us and learn to see in a new way.

Loren Eiseley was one of the great storytellers of our time. His stories not only reflect his training as an anthropologist (he taught for many years at the University of Pennsylvania), but his profound insight into the search for meaning that underlies all of human life. In *The Immense Journey* he tells a story that beautifully illustrates the connection between the world in which we live and the world of the Kingdom of God that lies just beyond our sight.

Eiseley describes leaving for work one day and heading out across a field near his house (as was his usual custom) to reach the train station a short distance away. On this particular morning the fog was so thick it was impossible to see any distance at all, requiring Eiseley to depend almost solely on his familiarity with the path. As he set out across the field he was stopped short by a sudden rush of wind and the sound of the most horrendous cawing he had ever heard. It was the cawing of an absolutely terrified crow.

How unusual for such a brave bandit as the crow to be so terrified. And then Eiseley realized what had happened. The crow, whose kingdom is normally high above the world of humans, was confused by the fog, and was suddenly confronted by what it thought was the most frightening menace it could possibly conceive of—an air-walking man.

"What had happened," Eiseley reflected, "was that in the fog my world and the world of the crow had interpenetrated, and neither of us would ever be the same again. We had come to believe in the miraculous, knowing in an unforgettable way that things are not always what they seem."[1]

I use Eiseley's story to illustrate what I believe to be the fundamental connection between prayer and the Kingdom of God. You cannot see one without the other. Prayer is the language of the Kingdom. It is the means by which we enter the world of the Spirit that is both within us and beyond our sight. Prayer is the source of our capacity for discernment—the gift that makes it possible for us to see with head and heart the Kingdom that is beyond us, amongst us, and within us.

Rabbi Abraham Joshua Heschel writes about what lies behind this gift of discernment:

Emotion is an important component of prayer, but the primary presupposition is conviction. If conviction is missing, if the presence of God is a myth, then prayer to God is a delusion. The source of prayer . . . is an insight rather than an emotion. It is the insight into the mystery of reality; it is, first of all, the sense of the ineffable that enables us to pray. As long as we refuse to take notice of what is beyond our sight, beyond our reason, as long as we are blind to the mystery of being, the way to pray is closed to us. If the rising of the sun is but a daily routine of nature there is no reason for us to praise the Lord for the sun and for the life we live.[2]

THE WAY WE PRAY REFLECTS THE WAY WE LIVE

The Chilean theologian Segundo Galilea has written that "Authentic Christian contemplation . . . transforms contemplatives into prophets and militants into mystics."[3] These provocative words have haunted me ever since I read them. They make clear in dramatic fashion the profound connection that exists between the way we pray and the way we live. Most of us *live* cautiously because we *pray* cautiously—a problem I would like to explore in what follows. "To be a fool for Christ's sake," to use Paul's phrase, implies the discovery of a radical kind of inner freedom that enables us to perceive life in a new way. According to Elizabeth O'Connor, writing out of her experience at the Church of the Saviour in Washington, D.C., "Every inward work requires an outward expression or it comes to naught. In fact, it may even fracture us further, widening the split between what we inwardly subscribe to and what we outwardly do. . . . 'Being' and 'doing' complete each other, as do 'staying' and 'going.' "[4]

This sense of connection between inner growth and outer change permeates the Christian understanding of reality. St. Paul was an activist of the first order. Every time he entered a new place he created major disruptions, but his activism was the fruit of the relationship he enjoyed with the living Christ. The great hymns of praise that seem to burst out in epistle after epistle are a testimony to the reality of this relationship. The ministries of Mother Teresa in the slums of Calcutta or of Martin Luther King in the streets of Montgomery, or of the countless people whose faith has touched your life and mine and indeed has affected the life of the world are expressions of lived prayer. These people went deep enough in prayer to embrace life with some degree of abandon. These inner experiences literally drove them in ministry to others.

THREE MOVEMENTS IN THE LIFE OF PRAYER

In the work of prayer, there are three interrelated movements that help us maintain and deepen the connection between inner growth and outer change. At the risk of oversimplification, let me refer to them as the movement of the self *toward* God, the movement *in* God, and the movement *through* God to embrace his creation. For each of these movements, the Spirit is at work moving us beyond our natural caution toward a new vision of reality. Our resistance to movement is the greatest problem most of us face in prayer. It is not that we do not pray; it is rather that we stop short of what is possible, and atrophy in our inwardness. The Gospel, of course, offers something more.

Look, if you will, at the movement in prayer *toward* God. The gift of faith, however it is received, activates this movement in all of us. To describe this movement we use such words as search or quest or exploration—meaning, of course, our response to the life of holiness, in all its many forms. In Frederick Buechner's *Godric*, there is a beautiful description of what this kind of prayer is about:

What's prayer? It's shooting shafts into the dark. What mark they strike, if any, who's to say? It's reaching for a hand you cannot touch. The silence is so fathomless that prayers like plummets vanish into the sea. You beg. You whisper. You load God down with empty praise. You tell him sins that he already knows full well. You seek to change his changeless will. Yet Godric prays the way he breathes, for else his heart would wither in his breast. Prayer is the wind that fills his sail. Else waves would dash him on the rocks, or he would drift with windless tides, and sometimes, by God's grace, a prayer is heard.[5]

TOWARD GOD

Movement in prayer *toward* God is not just the way we pray when we are beginning—when we are tentative and not sure—or even when we are desperate and can only cry out in the hope that someone will hear. Movement toward God is also a way of discovering our continuous encounter with the One who stands always beyond us as Creator and Judge. The One who is always Holy Other evokes from us not feelings of familiarity and comfort, but feelings of awe and wonder and adoration where we are faced with our own limitations. Without this, the sense of the immanence of God, that is, God in us, loses the tension needed to turn us outward or to push us beyond where we would normally choose to go, either in thought or in deed.

In the past few years there has been a lot of attention given in the Church to St. Paul's teaching on the gifts of the Spirit. This attention has been the source not only of widespread renewal throughout the Church, but also a heightened sense of the ministry in which we all share. What is needed to balance this emphasis is a recovery of the sense of what it means to stand before him who is always outside us and beyond us. The place to begin, I would suggest, is with a renewed acquaintance with the God who revealed himself to the prophets—the God of Isaiah and Jeremiah and Amos and Hosea. The movement of prayer toward God leads us always to a point of discomfort where the holiness and demands of God are experienced in a new way. When the prophet Isaiah was confronted by the awesome power of God, he not only experienced forgiveness, but also new direction and new motivation for his life. "Whom can I send, who will go for me?" was God's question. "Here I am, send me," was Isaiah's reply. The Holy One whom we call God can be experienced but never fully comprehended. He is the God of justice and mercy who calls us always to account.

IN GOD

But the movement of prayer is also *in* God. As Henry Nouwen writes, "Prayer, therefore, is God's breathing in us, by which we become part of the intimacy of God's inner life and by whom we are born anew."[6] This second movement of prayer is not so much about forming words or entering into conversation with God—although it might involve this—as it is about being in tune with God. It invokes stillness, inner quiet, and enough trust to let go so that our breath and our thoughts and our inmost sighs are caught up in the rhythm of God's life both in us and in the world. "Spirit of God, breathe through me." We can pray *in* God standing on a street corner waiting for the light to change, sitting in our office waiting for an appointment, or in the quiet of our home. For the Christian this is the way of prayer that sustains us, but it is also a way of praying that will lead us into a new experience of the world. The deeper we move in God, the more profound is the realization of our solidarity with the human family of which we are a part.

I shall never forget seeing a man rising from prayer in the midst of a retreat with tears streaming down his cheeks. "I have just discovered," he said, "what it means to say that the Russians are my brothers and sisters. It means that they can never be my enemy." The most profound motivation for peace does not come from our need for survival or fear of nuclear annihilation, but in the discovery of our solidarity with the human family for which Christ died. The movement of prayer in God—if we are not stuck—will ultimately lead us to say with the Lord Jesus, "*Our* Father, who art in heaven, hallowed be thy name." For to say "our" is to acknowledge our solidarity with others in Christ.

THROUGH GOD

Lastly, prayer is also movement *through* God to embrace his creation. Prayer is the language of the Kingdom of God. Like any kingdom, the Kingdom of God has its own language, its own customs, its own way of living together. When Jesus speaks he speaks the language of the Kingdom. His words are an expression of a vision he embodies in his own life. When John the Baptist was languishing in prison and beginning to doubt his own vision of the new age, Jesus sent him this message: "Go back and tell John what you see and hear," he told John's disciples, "the blind see again, and the lame walk, lepers are cleansed, and the deaf hear, and the dead are raised to life and the Good News is proclaimed to the poor, and happy is the man who does not lose faith in me" (Matt. 11:4–6).

The movement through God to embrace the world is that movement in prayer which produces in us a new set of eyes by which to view the world and the motivation to respond in love to what we see. This, of course, is the transformation—the renewing of our minds—that Paul talks about in the Letter to the Romans. It stirs in us the thirst for righteousness, and a deepened capacity for companionship. It invokes praying with compassion and praying for compassion. I have a friend who keeps a notebook with plastic frames for holding photographs. At the beginning of each week he clips pictures and headlines from the newspaper or from one of the news magazines and places them in the book of frames. He begins his meditation each day—which is sometimes short and sometimes long—by focusing on one of those frames. One day it might be a picture of a tiny child caught in a war that has exploded somewhere in the world. Another day, it might be a picture of the President or some other world leader. In prayer he seeks to become aware of what is before him so that at the depths of his heart he might for the moment through the connecting power of the Spirit experience what he sees. This is a powerful form of meditation prayer because it allows us to bring the vision of the Kingdom to bear on the realities of the world we live in—and then to embrace what we see as those called to share in the ministry of Christ.

Frederick Buechner relates a poignant story about moving through God to embrace the world in his autobiography, *The Sacred Journey*. He tells about going to visit his mother in New York from nearby New Jersey, where he was teaching. Just as he was about to sit down to a lovely dinner the phone rang for him. In a broken voice a friend and teaching colleague told him that he had just received word that his mother and father and sister had just been in an automobile accident and were not expected to live. Would he come? Buechner postponed making a decision, saying he would call the friend back; but before he did, his friend called to say *never mind*, and apologized profusely for his request. This is what Buechner writes:

My mother's apartment by candlelight was haven and home and shelter from everything in the world that seemed dangerous and a threat to my peace. And my friend's broken voice on the phone was a voice calling me out into that dangerous world not simply for his sake, as I suddenly saw it, but for my sake. . . . To journey for the sake of saving our own lives is little by little to cease to live in any sense that really matters, even to ourselves, because it is only by journeying for the world's sake—even when the world bores and sickens and scares you half to death—that little by little we start to come alive. It was not a conclusion that came to me in time. It was a conclusion from beyond time which came to me. God knows I have never been any good at following the road it pointed me to, but at least, by grace, I glimpsed the road and saw that it was the only one worth travelling.[7]

The movement of the Spirit in prayer is always to lead us beyond our own limited horizon to a new dimension of encounter with the world. This is how we know the degree of our responsiveness to the Spirit. Prayer moves us along toward a deeper but tougher experience of God; prayer moves us in God to experience the rhythm of his life. As hard as that is to believe, it is true. And prayer leads us *through* God and *in* God to touch and be touched by the world's pain. This is the invitation and the promise of prayer—that language by which we live and breathe in God's world, which, of course, is our world as well. Through the life of prayer, which for each of us has its own particularities, we share in and are grasped by the rhythms of holiness.

> Spirit of God, breathe through us and let us see.
> Spirit of God, love through us and set us free.
> Spirit of God, live through us that we might live in thee.

Work, Vocation, and Integrity

6.

Two plays appeared on Broadway recently that dealt with a similar theme from quite different perspectives. In a new production of Arthur Miller's classic, *Death of a Salesman*, we could see the agony of a man for whom the world of work has lost its meaning. Willie Loman, the salesman, was a man without a center. As the play comments, "He never knew who he was."

David Mamet's Pulitzer Prize-winning play, *Glengarry Glen Ross*, looks at the same problem from a different context. It reflects a significant shift in the way we have come to view reality since the 1940s, when Miller's play was first produced. There is the same agonizing appraisal of the lostness present in so much of our everyday working world, but it is a lostness that is more imbedded in the structures of society than in the individuals who make it up. The pain is the same, but the context and the source are different. Roma, the real estate salesman, describes this in a moving soliloquy addressed to another salesman he refers to as Machine (which in itself is descriptive):

I swear, it's not a world of men—it's not a world of men, Machine—it's a world of clock watches, bureaucrats, officeholders—

There's no adventure to it. (Pause) Dying breed. Yes it is. (Pause) We are members of a dying breed.[1]

This difference in perspective is a significant one for the way in which the Church understands vocation and the call to holiness. Salvation—the calling into being of God's New Creation—involves more than any individual relationship to God. It involves also the work of the Spirit within and amongst the structures of society releasing these structures from the destructive power of corporate human sin. In one sense both plays describe human life untouched by the holiness of God. The world we see portrayed is a world where the vision of God's Kingdom is obscured. Therefore to speak of the call to holiness, or of salvation, or of Christian vocation in solely personal terms is to limit our response to the action of God present in the world in which we live.

Not long ago I had the good fortune to spend some time with James Rouse, the developer and planner who now is world famous for his work in renewing the harbor area of the city of Baltimore. During our conversation Rouse talked about the importance of the Christian faith in his life and of his experience at the Church of the Saviour in Washington, D.C. He then went on to describe a visit he had made to the Soviet Union that, in many ways, changed the direction of his life.

As a member of an American delegation of architects and builders, Rouse visited schools of architecture and various housing projects throughout Russia that were pointed out as the best in contemporary Soviet architecture and building. He recalled being impressed by the caliber of the architectural schools he saw and the high degree of personal creativity that was expressed. What shocked him, however, was the poor quality and lack of imagination expressed in Soviet housing—the product of these schools. He asked his hosts how they accounted for the discrepancy. Their reply was clear and to the point: In the United States, they observed, the major focus of architecture and building in the housing arena is on luxury housing for the few. In the Soviet Union the concern is to provide more economic housing for the many. Rouse said he suddenly realized that until American architects and builders could deal more adequately with housing for the poor, they had nothing to say to the Soviets. "I vowed then," Rouse said, "that I would spend the rest of my life trying to address this very human challenge."

Rouse now chairs the Enterprise Foundation, which draws on the profits of the Enterprise Development Company to research and provide more adequate housing for the urban poor. I don't know any of the details of James Rouse's life, nor any of the conscious relationship that exists between his faith and his work; but when he spoke I knew I was being addressed by a man whose life had been shaped by a clear sense of vocation. Somewhere in his life Rouse had been touched by the holiness of God and his life began to reflect in part the vision of the Kingdom that God's holiness embodies.

THE MEANING OF VOCATION

It is more and more my conviction that before we can speak of ministry in the local church, it is necessary to help people understand the nature of the Christian calling that undergirds it. Until we are able to see our lives in vocational terms—that is, as a lived out expression of what we believe—we will continue to respond to the invitation to share in the ministry of Christ as a request to take on another job in the midst of an already overcrowded life.

The English word vocation comes from the Latin word *vocare*, which means "to call." We therefore speak of a vocation as a calling, implying that by using our lives in a particular way we are contributing toward God's purpose for the world. To speak of our work as a vocation or of a married or single life as being a vocation is a way of saying that the way we live and what we do are to the best of our knowledge expressions of God's will for our lives. A vocation is a calling from God—discerned consciously—to use our gifts for a particular purpose. It therefore implies a sense of direction and purpose and a high degree of dedication.

Vocation is an important word in the Christian vocabulary, but unfortunately the way it is used is not always helpful. In the Christian Church we speak quite readily of someone having a vocation to the ordained ministry, but are less clear about the vocational aspects of other walks of life. We imply by this that vocation to the ordained ministry is the one true Christian vocation from which all others derive. This way of speaking not only contributes to the sense of separation that exists between clergy and laity—a separation that badly hampers the carrying out of the Church's mission—but it contributes to the confusion that is reflected in the lives of so many clergy regarding the distinction between role and work.

Every Christian has a vocation. We are called to share in the ministry of Jesus Christ *in* and *through* the world. In the Sacrament of Baptism this call is incarnated, giving us both a clear *identity* in the world and a sense of purpose about what our lives are ultimately for. Sharing in the ministry of Jesus Christ involves living in the world as an expression of the holiness we see in him—a holiness expressed through his compassion, his concern for justice (righteousness), and through his healing and reconciling presence in the world. The relationship he offers to us—when entered into with seriousness—results in those qualities we see in him being expressed through us, sometimes even despite ourselves. We cannot, therefore, limit this expression to a particular profession or a particular role or a particular job. Being called to the priesthood involves sharing in the ministry of Jesus Christ in a particular way. A priest is identified by the Church to be a sign of Christ's presence and ministry for others. But being a priest also involves doing a job, a job that, like all other jobs, sometimes blocks vocational expression rather than enhances it. The distinction is an important one. When a priest consistently absents himself or herself from family commitments on the grounds that the job takes priority because it is his or her vocation, he or she is denying the fact that if we are married, family life is as important an arena for expressing our vocation as is the work we do for the Church. Neither is more sacred than the other.

Christian vocation involves the whole of our lives since it is the way we live out the implications of our baptism. We do this specifically by exercising our gifts in particular ministries. We are always acting in the world as healers and reconcilers and advocates of justice except, of course, when blocked by the sin that is within all of us; but there are times and places when our vocational commitment leads us into specific ministries that might be very short-lived or last a lifetime. It is, of course, a plus when these specific expressions of ministry coincide with our job. But it is also important to remember that for many people the job is not the primary focus of ministry, and it does no good for the Church to romanticize beyond what reality can bear.

In *The Ethics of Freedom* Jacques Ellul insists that in the interest of vocation, work must be viewed in far more relative terms than we tend to see it—including work in the Church. This does not mean that we have to diminish the importance of the work we do—if indeed we do feel it to be important—but rather accept the fact that all work is not necessarily fulfilling, nor does it necessarily contribute to the common good. "If then, we cannot unify our life or incarnate our Christian vocation," writes Ellul, "if we are brought by the technological society into the harsh condition of relative work that has neither value nor ultimate meaning, then we obviously have to discover a form of activity which will express our Christian vocation and thus be an incarnation of our faith."

Ellul continues in what I find to be a particularly helpful analysis:

Since our responsibility is to the world this cannot be a purely inward affair nor a good work in the ordinary meaning of the term, e.g., a work of charity. This vocation must find expression in an action: an action that will have social and collective impact which in one way or another can change the form of the world in which we are; an action that has to be gratuitous even though it retains the features of seriousness, competence, continuity, and invention that we attribute to real work. It seems to me that only thus can this kind of activity express vocation. As vocation is free and an expression of grace, so this activity must be free in return.[2]

Christian vocation is expressed in many ministries, all of which reflect our participation in the one ministry of Jesus Christ in and to the world. For some these ministries will be primarily job related, for others they will take different forms—some through the institutional church, others through other settings. We can speak of what we do as ministries because in some recognizable (but not necessarily obvious) way they reflect something of the holiness of Christ and make (in Ellul's words) "a social and collective impact" on "the form of the world in which we are," regardless of how small an impact this may seem to be. Ellul's criteria of *seriousness*, *competence*, *continuity*, and *invention* are qualities by which we might judge the degree of commitment we are prepared to make

—qualities that are as important for a volunteer job in our parish church or community service organizations as they are for a nationwide scheme of urban renewal. The issue is how can our Christian vocation best be expressed in what we do, and how can our life in Christ count for something that will make a difference in God's sight.

One of the greatest misconceptions ever foisted on the Church is the idea that when we speak about a priest being "set apart," we mean being set apart from the laity. I think this is a misreading of the biblical witness. A priest, as a representative of the total Christian community, is not through ordination set apart from the laity, or for that matter from anyone—including other clergy—but rather from a view of the world that gives greater value to power and separateness than it does to love and human solidarity in Christ. Christian ministry is by its very nature mutual ministry. When the Lord sent out the seventy, he sent them out two by two. Mutuality in ministry is the recognition that I need you, you need me, and we both need the power of the living Christ if our ministries are to be fulfilled.

VOCATION AND OUR APPROACH TO WORK

In an article entitled "Personality, Faith Development, and Work Attitudes," John Vogelsang makes interesting use of the Baruch-Segel study of how men and women relate career to family. Although the descriptive terms used in the study sound somewhat simplistic, they nevertheless raised some interesting questions about the relationship between our sense of personal integrity and the way we understand Christian vocation.

Baruch identifies five thematic orientations to career and family, which she defines as: (1) purposeful breadwinner, (2) oppressed breadwinner, (3) role polarizers, (4) conflicted, and (5) happy harmonizers. In summarizing these thematic orientations, Vogelsang writes:

The *purposeful breadwinners* are concerned with the needs of their families. Work is accepted as an instrument to satisfy their needs. Work is not a means of self-actualization but a means of providing. The *oppressed breadwinner* views work as a bitter experience. Their families compensate, but they consider their families the only reason they are working. They feel unchallenged by work and feel they are sacrificing themselves *for* the sake of others. The *role polarizers* invest themselves heavily in either work or family. One or the other becomes their whole life. The *conflicted* feel work demands interfere wtih their family role. They derive satisfaction from *both* and feel pulled between them. The *happy harmonizers* enjoy their families *and* their work. They feel a sense of well-being and contentment about their lives. Baruch offers these five dimensions as a way to characterize how people perceive work and family roles. She does not imply that there is a developmental aspect to the attitudes.[3]

The question we must ask as Christians is not which of these is better. Rather, given a particular orientation to work and family— an orientation, I suspect, that also has parallels for single and divorced people—we must ask what vocational aspects are present. If a divorced mother who is raising two children expresses herself as an oppressed breadwinner in the only job she can get, how do we heighten the vocational aspects of her commitment to give her children the best that she can while helping her manage the stress of her job? And how can role polarizers be helped to see that *total* investment in job or family can do as much to distort vocation as to enhance it, simply because it requires so much denial to maintain?

Christian vocation does not demand that work and family be happily harmonized—although we can rejoice when such is the case. What is required of us is awareness of choices we make and the impact of those choices on others. Christian vocation in some cases might demand that, for the sake of personal integrity and the Gospel values we profess, we must choose to live in disharmony rather than run the risk of losing our true selves.

VOCATION AND INTEGRITY

Christian vocation is the way our lives express holiness, for it is a call to live our lives not as manipulators of power, but in seeking the empowerment of the powerless. The vocation of Jesus was to live in the world as humanity's servant. To share his ministry is to share his servanthood. This understanding is fundamental to Christian ministry. The servant image in the New Testament is not an image of weakness or subservience. It is an image that reflects the meaning of power put to its rightful use—be it on a personal level, a corporate level, or even on an international level.

Servanthood in the biblical sense can never emerge out of a need to control or dominate—for control is but a way of dealing with our fear of losing or of being made more vulnerable. Servanthood is the fruit of Grace—the discovery that the meaning of life lies in our ability to give it to others, which takes place in community.

As Elizabeth O'Connor states so eloquently: "There is no higher achievement in all the world than to be a person in community, and this is the call of every Christian. We are to be builders of liberating communities which free love in us and free love in others."[4] No act of ministry is any more important, nor is there any setting where it cannot be exercised—be it teaching children in public school or in church school class or in working with others to decide a question of corporate policy.

Christian vocation is a description of a life in which power is exercised in obedience to that vision embodied in the ministry of Jesus Christ. It involves being clear about when we say "yes" and when we say "no," and to whom, for vocation is expressed in *being* and *doing* by the grace of God what we say we believe in. It is to this kind of inner integrity that we are called, but it is an integrity that comes not as the result of our own effort alone, but as the fruit of our relationship to Jesus Christ.

To live in response to God's call to holiness involves a commitment to growing self-awareness—paying attention, if you will, to that movement toward wholeness that exists in all of us—but in the context of a vision of what human life is about and what our lives in particular are for. In describing the meaning of Christian vocation, Frederick Buechner has written: "The place God calls you to is the place where your deep gladness and the world's deep hunger meet."[5] I don't know how it could be said any better.

Education for Holiness

7.

The theological task of the educational and pastoral ministry of the Christian Church is to awake in the people of God a thirst for holiness that opens them to the transforming power of God's unmeasured grace. Holiness, as we have sought to define it, is a word rooted in Scripture that describes what happens to us when the Kingdom of God impinges on our experience. There is no way we can produce holiness, but we can help to create an environment in which holiness is seen as something that is both significant and possible for men and women of today. It is to the "how" of such a task that we now turn our attention.

Thomas Groome, in his extremely thoughtful book *Christian Religious Education*, offers a definition of the educational task of the church that provides a useful focus in building an environment in which the seeds of holiness can flourish and grow. "Christian religious education," he writes, "is a political activity with pilgrims in time that deliberately and intentionally attends with them to the activity of God in our present, to the story of the Christian faith community, and to the Vision of God's Kingdom, the seeds of which are already among us."[1] What I find significant in Groome's definition, and with the method of "shared praxis" through which his definition is actually lived out, is the emphasis placed on seeing the present in the light of the Kingdom as it impinges upon us from the future and demands of us moral choice.

In speaking of the educational task of the church, the idea of environment is particularly important. Programs and classes don't educate by themselves. Education occurs as the result of the impact of total community upon human consciousness. Even at our best the environment Christian community provides is but a very small portion of people's total experience; therefore it must be developed with infinite care. One fundamental principle that is essential to effective education in the life of the church is the recognition that everything that goes on educates. *When* spontaneity and self-expression are encouraged, we are teaching something quite specific about life in Christ; *when* relationships between people are formal and distant, we are saying something quite different. The way the church is organized, the relationships that exist between clergy and laity and between the community as a whole (including relationships between the generations) are the stuff from which education takes place. The basic educational question for any Christian community therefore is, "What are we expressing by what we do?" and "How does this contrast with what we *want* to express?" And, of course, there is the action question that follows: "How then do we close the gap?"

The following story illustrates my point. A friend of mine recently moved to a new town and he and his wife joined the local Episcopal church. He chose this church because he was told by its members how friendly a place it was. Although my friends are rather outgoing types, they found it impossible to get into conversation with anyone. After three or four months they had made contact with the members of only one other family, and they too were new. The congregation was not made up of uncaring people, but there was a discrepancy between what the members understood themselves to be and how they were actually experienced by others. What could have been done to rectify this? To improve the environment, each member of a congregation needs to become aware of gaps in his or her perceived understanding and respond to them with real change.

In creating an environment that deepens the thirst for holiness, five areas need particular emphasis:

1. expanding the imagination so that people can begin to see more clearly beyond the obvious
2. helping people to encounter the surprises of Scripture
3. enabling people to frame life-questions
4. providing opportunities for voluntary displacement
5. deepening the inner life of people in ways that connect them to the intercessary community of which they are a part.

1. EXPANDING THE IMAGINATION

Mark Helprin's remarkable *Winter's Tale*, a novel about the pursuit of what is referred to as the "Golden City"—the city where justice reigns—is also a novel in which timelessness has a way of impinging on the present. The central character is an orphan who arrived on the shores of New Jersey as a tiny infant and was found much like Moses in the bullrushes. During the course of the novel he meets and falls in love with Beverly Penn, a beautiful young woman who is slowly dying of tuberculosis, but who possesses qualities that invoke new ways of perception in others:

Peter Lake rode Athansor at a lope over snow-covered streets with the north wind against him. It was very cold, and the wind put icicles on his mustache. Though the doctor hadn't known that the woman Peter Lake loved was in the midst of dying, his advice could not have been more appropriate or more painful to hear, especially because it echoed what Beverly had said not long before in the second (though by far not the last) delirium in which he was to see her. "I'm just like you," she had told him. "I come from another age. But there are many things that we must take care of now." . . .

If she were correct, it would explain why the world sometimes seemed to be a stage behind which was a strangely benevolent, superior, and indifferent power. The suffering of the innocent would be accounted for, if, in ages to come or ages that had been, the reasons for everything were revealed and balances were evened. It would explain destiny, and coincidence, and his image of the city as if he had been looking from high above at a living creature with a pelt of dusky light. It would explain the things that called to Beverly from a far distance and a far time. It would suggest that Athansor, who could leap high into the air, was leaping toward something he already knew. It would explain the strong feeling Peter Lake had that every action in the world had eventual consequences and would never be forgotten, as if it were entered in a magnificent ledger of unimaginable complexity. He thought that it might explain freedom, memory, transfiguration, and justice—though he did not know how.[2]

Before I was half-way through Helprin's novel I realized I was experiencing something quite remarkable. I would read at night and fall asleep with images of the Kingdom dancing in my consciousness. I do not suggest that *Winter's Tale* will have this same effect on everyone, but for me Helprin's imagination and my readiness met.

There is a great need in religious education to enable people to encounter the aesthetic dimensions of life in ways that expand their consciousness. As part of our program in spiritual direction at the General Theological Seminary we have taken classes to the Cloisters, the museum of medieval art in New York City, to meditate on the images presented to them in some of the great classics of Christian art. We in the Church need to talk with each other more about plays and movies and words and poetry and music and dance. "Aesthetic experience and sacramental experience," writes the theologian Anthony Padovano, "deal with the physical world directly but beneath the surface experience. They transform the vision we have of the world which engages us. The artist reveals the glory within an otherwise unexpected experience. We encounter the familiar charged with mystery."[3]

To be concerned about holiness is to be open to this mystery, and to create an environment where this is possible. Worship and the arts are places to begin—or, as the case may be, to continue.

2. THE SURPRISES OF SCRIPTURE

The second area of emphasis has to do with the way we apprehend the study of Scripture in the life of the Church. What is needed, I believe, along with pure exposure, is an attitude of expectancy toward what the Bible contains. We need to learn to look for the surprises. The stories of Jesus' ministry contained in the Gospel are full of surprises—Bartimaeus is forced to take responsibility for himself; the man who worked less is paid more; in a very masculine world, it is a group of women who first see and bear witness to the resurrected Lord.

A place to begin, as I have suggested earlier, might be with the prophets and the parables, since in so many ways both deal with the coming of the Kingdom. The question we ask is simple; What is it about this passage of the Bible that suggests a new way of viewing the world, or forces us to see differently? Little children can be taught to look for surprises—in Scripture, and in the world around. Holy expectancy, I would like to suggest, is itself a sign of the Kingdom.

3. FRAMING LIFE-QUESTIONS

In his *Letters to a Young Poet* Rainer Maria Rilke suggested that the way to perceive the mystery that surrounds human experience is to concentrate not so much on finding the answers to life's riddles as to take time to frame the right questions.

Be patient toward all that is unsolved in your heart and try to love the *questions* themselves like locked rooms and like books that are written in a foreign language. Do not now seek the answers, which cannot be given you because you would not be able to live them. And the point is, to live everything. *Live* the questions now. Perhaps you will then gradually, without noticing it, live along some distant day into the answer.[4]

As we live into the questions the answers will emerge, but they will emerge deep within us. What we are talking about, of course, are life-questions—questions that enable us to see. I have often found it helpful at the end of a class or discussion to ask people to be still for a moment and let a question emerge as a result of what has been happening to them in the class. "What are the unresolved questions," we might ask, "that remain within me and need to be nurtured?"

On another level we need to help one another ask questions that enable us to get a clearer perspective on what for us is most true. I referred earlier to the need to be able to ask questions of the psychological disciplines about implied meanings as they relate to our faith. In approaching this, the following questions might be a place to begin. They are questions that might be asked of theological statements as well:

1. Is this a vision of humanity which softens our edges and opens us to new experience, or does it close us off from new ways of seeing?
2. Does it take seriously the transcendent dimension of reality and the need for the cultivation of our inner space?

3. Are the qualities of life present in this vision and the values that derive from them compatible with what we see in Jesus Christ?
4. Does it take seriously the power of human sin in a way that opens to us the reality of the Cross and the world's need of God's saving Grace?
5. Does it open to us that vision of the world implicit in Jesus' proclamation of the Kingdom of God?
6. What is the explicit or implicit fruit of human growth and is this compatible with our growing in Christ?

Many more questions, of course, could be added. What is important, however, is to frame questions that open us up to the possibility of dialogue, rather than premature closure. Our aim is not to prove a point, but to seek the truth.

4. VOLUNTARY DISPLACEMENT

In 1965 I had the good fortune to be part of an educational project that took me to Japan and eventually to Hong Kong. While in Kowloon, that teeming city within the Hong Kong colony, I met a man who ranks high on my list of the most unforgettable people I have ever met. My friend was Eurasian and a deeply committed Christian who had developed a ministry to the thousands of unemployed men who had come over the borders of China searching for work. To help house these people the Church had established a number of hostels for which my friend was responsible. His task was to reach out to these people in the name of Christ, offering whatever support he could. Day after day, he recounted, he would go into the hostels seeking to make contact, but there was no response. Every effort was met with suspicion and guarded silence until one day something quite remarkable happened.

As he went into one of the hostels he discovered that the latrines had been stopped up and raw sewage had been spilling out on the floor. Immediately, my friend grabbed a mop and went to work. Before long he was joined by one of the residents, then another, then another. As they worked they talked, and the barrier was broken. "It was so obvious," he said to me later, "I don't know why I had not seen it before. It was not that we worked to-gether. This was not new. It ws that for the first time they saw me as their servant. This is what made the difference. It was different because in voluntarily putting myself in their place, I saw *them* differently and was able to enter their world in a new way."

Voluntary displacement is an ancient spiritual discipline that involves choosing to place yourself in a world other than your own in order to experience the world from another perspective. If genuine connections are made with those whose lives you share, there is the possibility that you will encounter the Kingdom in ways you never suspected. Such displacement can be as common-place as a volunteer job in the summer or as difficult as learning a new language in order to be open to the nuances of another culture.

In his book *¡Gracias!* Henri Nouwen tells of what happened in his life as a result of his decision to spend time among the poor of Bolivia and Peru.

Latin America offers us the image of the suffering of Christ. The poor we see every day, the stories about deportation, torture, and murder we hear every day, and the undernourished children we touch every day, reveal to us the suffering of Christ hidden within us. When we allow this image of the suffering Christ within us to grow into full maturity, then ministry to the poor and oppressed becomes a real possibility, because then we can indeed hear, see and touch him within us as well as among us.[5]

We might add that we experience also the mystery of the holiness of God.

5. WORSHIP AND THE INNER LIFE

There is no way we can speak of cultivating the thirst for holi-ness without speaking of the ways in which people are invited into the life of prayer and worship. There is no doubt that for many people serious prayer is difficult and unfamiliar, but it is nevertheless the doorway to the Kingdom.

It is my experience that worship takes on a new dimension for people when they are enabled to move beyond the consumer mentality that is so characteristic of our culture to a sense of being an integral part of a community that extends me beyond myself. The question we ask when we begin to make this shift is no longer, "What does this experience of worship do for me?" but rather, "What out of my experience do I bring to it?" Central to this understanding is the realization that in Christian worship, and particularly in the celebration of Eucharist, we share in the mystery of Jesus Christ's intercession on behalf of the world.

Christian worship is built on the fundamental theological assertion that as the Body of Christ we exist not for ourselves, but on behalf of the world. We gather together in worship to serve as leaven in the world, praying on behalf of those who cannot or will not pray themselves. In the Christian Church the Eucharistic liturgy is an embodiment of the Kingdom vision. In it we share in the self-offering of Christ for the entire human family. Therefore the care and preparation given to the intercessions of the people are critical to the integrity of worship. We gather not primarily as individuals to nurture our own relationship to God, but as a community of those baptized into Christ, each with a place and each with a particular work of prayer to do in order to complete the whole.

I know of a family who, when they cannot worship themselves, make a special point to ask someone to pray on their behalf lest their absence diminish the intercessory work of their parish community. I know also of a parish where Sunday intercessions are led by rotating intercessory teams whose task it is to lift up before God particular concerns for which the parish intends to pray, with the understanding that the intensity and clarity of their prayer will by the grace of God make a difference. I know of another parish where the ministries of the scattered congregation—that is, ministries in the world at large—are identified and prayed for in a consistent manner. And, of course, as we add our own experience, the list of examples of what it means to be an intercessory community grows larger.

Education for worship is education for holiness, for in no other place in the life of a parish is the reality of that Kingdom that lies just beyond our sight any more present. Worship, in whatever setting it takes place, is an act of symbolic encounter. Although much is obviously rational and reflective, much is not, which leads me to believe that it is the *environment* of worship maybe even more than its content that has the strongest educational impact. The movement, the dramatic emphasis as the story of Redemption unfolds, the deep silences, the sense of participation and belonging, the subliminal connections—these have as much impact on us as what is said. The point is, if we are serious about education for holiness, this seriousness is reflected in the care given to what happens when the community gathers to share in Jesus' prayer for the coming of the Kingdom.

WHOLENESS AND HOLINESS

Education for holiness is about building connections between what we know about ourselves and the mystery of the Kingdom as it impinges upon us. It is about compassion, and righteousness, and companionship, as we, with others, journey in faith. Holiness, once it is glimpsed, transforms our self-understanding by creating in us a thirst that will not go away. "Strive for peace with all people," wrote the author of the Letter to the Hebrews (12:14), "and for the holiness without which no one will see the Lord." This is an invitation to open our eyes in order to see things we have never seen before.

In *The Magnificent Defeat* Frederick Buechner tells of sitting in the corridor of a hospital after the patients are all asleep, and suddenly noticing that there is another person sitting close by, a stranger. The silence between them becomes very deep—so deep, he says, that you can almost hear it—but the mystery of who he is and who the stranger is remains hidden. Finally, on sudden impulse, he speaks—and before long a connection is made, and "a little bridge is built, and you meet on the bridge."[6]

Holiness is about building bridges—within ourselves, into Christ, and into the Kingdom that is now amongst us, and within us, and is yet still to come.

Epilogue: A Modern Parable

Once upon a time in a beautiful land far, far away, there was a king who was obsessed with finding ways to keep his country busy. Idleness, he was fond of saying, was the work of the devil. After much worry, and much study, he came up with a plan. At the moment of birth a tiny electronic receiver was to be implanted in everyone's brain—much like the headsets people wear while jogging—only invisible. Pretty soon the idea became so popular that *everyone* had a receiver, and soon having a receiver in one's head became the law of the land. Life became tuned to the music everyone heard on his or her receiver. And as the music became faster, people worked harder. But there was one problem: only one kind of music was played—and, of course, the king called the tune.

Before long, people all worked at the same fast pace, they walked in the same fast step, and they began to look more and more alike. One man, however, was an exception. When the pace got faster, he moved in quiet deliberation. When the people marched, he danced. He danced up one street and down the other with such utter joy that people were fascinated and began to seek him out. In a very short time, however, he was arrested and examined as the authorities sought to find out what made him so out of step. Like everyone else he had been given a receiver, but something had gone wrong. After a long investigation the secret became known. The man who danced had found a way to change the frequency of his receiver so that he could hear a different tune.

There is in Christianity a strain that echoes this parable. We speak of Christians being in the world but not *of* the world—a reflection, of course, of Jesus' own self-understanding. What this means is not that we don't take the world seriously, or that we are called to detach ourselves from the world's pain and suffering; rather it is just the opposite. We are called to embrace the world from a particular perspective. We are indeed invited to walk to a different tune. Clearly, this is not an invitation that is attractive to everyone. It becomes attractive when we begin to own the restlessness many of us feel about the direction (or more accurately, the lack of direction) in which our lives seem to be headed. Holiness becomes an attractive possibility when the Spirit touches us in such a way that we want our lives to really count for something. The thirst for holiness is the response that emerges within us when we discover that the center of our lives is nowhere near as focused and full as it might be and we yearn desperately for it to be filled. When this happens it is quite natural to ask, "How do we begin?"

THE PATHWAY TO HOLINESS

I would like to suggest five steps that I believe can help lead us more deeply into the holy life. The first three are essentially internal, and the latter two involve taking specific action. They are offered not as tasks to be accomplished, but as doors to be opened.

1. CLAIMING THE GIFT OF FAITH

There is contained in the Gospels a very well known and very explicit invitation to faith. "Ask and it will be given you," Jesus told his disciples, "seek and you will find; knock, and it will be opened to you. For every one who asks receives, and he who seeks finds, and to him who knocks it will be opened" (Matt. 7:7–11 and Luke 11:9–15). What is promised is not a ready-made solution to all of life's problems, or even absolute certainty about what the Christian faith claims to be true (and, of course, even this differs widely according to the tradition in which we stand). What is promised is a relationship to Jesus Christ—a connection that grounds our lives into a source of meaning and power that allows us to risk embracing all that we do not know with a degree of expectancy and trust. The context of Christian faith is the affirmation—the trust—that our relationship with Jesus Christ is in itself an experience of God and has creative and sustaining power. In this sense we can say that there is a difference between faith and belief.

Faith is the gift of God that embraces us and calls forth in us trust and an openness to the mystery of holiness. Belief is our response to this gift. It is our assent to the experience and teaching of the Christian community as this is filtered through our own experience and incorporated into our lives. When faith is solid, and continually nourished, it is possible for belief to be flexible and open-ended. This, I believe, is what Robinson is talking about when he speaks of having soft edges and a solid center.[1] This question is not an unimportant one. We live in a world where religion is more and more being seen as assent to "right belief" (depending, of course, on whose version of "right belief" we adopt). We see this in the resurgence of a kind of hostile fundamentalism in Islam, and we see it in our own country in the way Christianity is being presented in popular culture (mixed up with Americanism and political fervor). I believe that a case can be made—and indeed must be made—for an understanding of faith that builds community rather than divides it; and which, because it is rooted in trust rather than the need for certainty, is open and responsive to the wonder and mystery of the Kingdom.

2. ACCEPTING OURSELVES IN CHRIST

The great freedom we experience in Christ is awareness (itself a gift of faith) that our worth as a person does not ultimately depend on our own efforts, but in what Jesus Christ has done on our behalf. His offering of himself on the Cross as an act of love, love that included even those who were putting him to death, has the effect of drawing all humankind into *his* worth. And so, in the realization of this, Paul could proclaim, "If God is for us, who can be against us?" It is the Christian affirmation that God looks upon us only as we are reflected in Christ, which means that he sees us only as people who are forgiven.

We are most destructive of others when we are at war with ourselves. Those negative characteristics I see in others are all too often projections of those qualities I prefer not to see in myself. The pathway to holiness therefore, as has been said before, is a path that takes seriously the need for inner wholeness and opens us to the healing power of the Spirit from which inner wholeness comes.

Accepting ourselves in Christ is the fruit of the recognition that God's acceptance of us has already taken place. To know this in faith allows us to dare embrace the dark side of ourselves not as an enemy to be conquered, but as a friend to be healed and integrated into the center of our lives. Accepting ourselves involves self-affirmation (as opposed to selfishness) and a sense of appreciation for the many gifts we have been given—including the gift of life itself. Self-acceptance in Christ involves the recognition that we are not fully ourselves until we are centered in him. For as Christ lives in us, so are we also to live for others—and this is what holiness is about.

3. ACKNOWLEDGING OUR SOLIDARITY WITH OTHERS

Wholeness not only refers to psychic wholeness—"getting one's life together," as we hear it often said—but to the essential connectedness of God's world. Just as our intellectual and emotional life affects our physical health, and vice versa, so does the quality of life in one part of the globe affect the way people live in others. When we think war, or when we think of people as enemies, we release energy into the world that is as destructive as putting poison in drinking water. When Jesus spoke of seeking the Kingdom of God first (Matt. 6:33), he was talking about those fundamental attitudes with which we view the world and the people in it.

The pathway to holiness, by its very nature, leads us from individualistic religion to communal faith. The Christian faith is never a matter of relationship to God alone—*my* salvation, *my* individual problem, *my* conversion—but always my relationship to God *in community* and in solidarity with the world for whom Christ died. Faith in the Risen Christ moves us from "I" and "me" to "we" and "us." This is why I cannot rejoice in America's prosperity unless that prosperity is contributing to the well-being of the world at large. Faith is a matter of vision, of seeing the face of Christ in those whom the world chooses to overlook or even in those who hate us. The vision of the Kingdom is a vision of the world made whole. Whenever or wherever signs of this wholeness appear—a new peace effort, one community reaching out to another, food from one nation being made available to those in need—we encounter the holiness of God. Sometimes we see this holiness reflected in an individual, sometimes in a people; sometimes for a fleeting moment, sometimes for a generation. We see holiness in others when they are touched in some way by the reality of the Kingdom.

4. EMBRACING THE COMMUNITY OF FAITH

From time to time the question emerges (usually as a way of putting someone down), "can you be a Christian without going to church?" The problem with the question is that it puts the emphasis in the wrong place. The expression of faith in Christ is not so much a matter of going to church (as we go to a movie or watch television) as it is a matter of *being* the Church. Christian faith, as we have said, is by its nature communal. Our identity in Christ is not experienced in isolation, but as a people described by Paul as the Body of Christ. It is in community—"where two or three are gathered in my name, there am I in the midst of them" (Matt. 18:20)—that we experience life in Christ, and it is in an expression of this fundamental communal identity that we gather with other Christians for worship.

The pathway to holiness leads us to seek the community of others who share the same vision. Sometimes in an established congregation the vision of God's Kingdom is not readily apparent but is there nevertheless, expressed week after week in Word and Sacrament, and often in the lives of those we would least expect. Admittedly, Christian community is not always easy to find, nor is it easy to sustain. It is, nevertheless, the fruit of faith and the means by which we share in the ministry of Christ in the world.

5. WORKING FOR THE KINGDOM—ONE STEP AT A TIME

The gift of holiness, as we have seen, involves a change of consciousness in which our vision is enlarged and our perception sharpened. Holiness, therefore, is never static. It is a gift of energy and power keyed to a rhythm that permeates the universe. When we first experience this energy (sometimes also referred to as the gift of the Spirit, or as the Grace of God, or as new life in Christ) there is a tendency to take on everything. Signs of the Kingdom are everywhere and we can burn ourselves out unless the way we respond is grounded in solitude and taken one step at a time.

Although the specifics vary, the themes of the Kingdom are consistent. They involve concern for world peace and disarmament—"They shall beat their swords into ploughshares, and their spears into pruning forks, nation shall not lift up sword against nation, neither shall there be war any more" (Is. 2:4); for the poor and hungry—"go, sell what you possess and give it to the poor, and you will have treasure in heaven; and come, follow me" (Matt. 19:21); for justice—"Will not God see justice done to his chosen who cry out to him day and night? . . . I promise you, he will see justice done, and done speedily" (Luke 18:7–8); for reconciliation and the building of community—"all this is from God, who through Christ reconciled us to himself and gave us the ministry of reconciliation" (2 Cor. 5:18–19).

The pathway to holiness leads us to link ourselves in a serious way to a Kingdom value toward whose realization we are willing to commit our energy. Mahatma Gandhi and Martin Luther King were touched by holiness in their pursuit of justice through non-violence, clear Kingdom values. The holiness of Mother Teresa and Desmond Tutu is the holiness that emerges out of their compassion for the poor and oppressed. And there is holiness present in those who struggle for peace and the abolition of the threat of nuclear war. We can't do everything, but each of us can do something. What we do—what we pay attention to—depends, of course, on the tune we hear.

THE DANCE AS A METAPHOR OF HOLINESS

The Dancing Man, a beautiful book written for children by Ruth Bornstein, uses the image of the dance as a metaphor for life.[2]

What it describes, however, are signs of the Kingdom, unidentified but nevertheless clearly present. In this sense it offers to us the dance as a metaphor of holiness.

Once, in a poor village by the Baltic Sea, there lived an orphan boy named Joseph. When he was still very small, Joseph knew that life in the village was dreary and hard. No one laughed. No one danced. But Joseph saw that all around him the world danced. Fire danced in the hearth. Trees swayed in the wind. Clouds danced in the sky. . . .

And then, one evening, by the sea, Joseph met an old man with silver shoes who was indeed "dancing the waves."

The old man swept off his hat and bowed. "I'm the Dancing Man," he said, "and I have a gift for you."

The gift was a pair of silver shoes, and before long Joseph began to dance, taking the old man's place. He danced from village to village, and as he danced people responded. "An old woman gave him a flower, and Joseph danced with the flower." He met a young child who was ill and in pain, and as he danced the young girl smiled. He met a farmer and saw the sowing of the seeds and the ripening of the harvest. Wherever Joseph danced there was life, until the day came when he was old. And then one day he looked up and saw standing by the sea a young child, waiting, as long ago he had waited.

The boy drew near. Joseph knew the words to say. He swept off his hat and bowed. "I'm the Dancing Man," he said, "and I have a gift for you."

Holiness is wholeness transfigured. It sees all life in mysterious interconnection and bids us join in that dance which emerges in response to the rhythm of the Kingdom. Holiness is about compassion and righteousness, and companionship. It is a sign of a new world already begun yet still to be fulfilled. It begins in faith and is nourished by the imagination and wonder of that community of believers who dare to risk not knowing in order to know and live more deeply. The invitation to holiness is an invitation to join the dance with those who believe that the Kingdom of God is amongst us now.

So, dance, dance, wherever you may be;
I am the Lord of the Dance said he.
And I'll lead you all wherever you may be;
And I'll lead you all in the Dance said he.[3]

Notes

INTRODUCTION

1. Don Browning, "Pastoral Theology in a Pluralistic Age," *Pastoral Psychology* 29, No. 1 (Fall 1980): 24.
2. I have in mind such recent books as Alister Campbell's *Rediscovering Pastoral Care* (Philadelphia: Westminster, 1981); Gabriel Moran's *Religious Education Development: Images for the Future* (Minneapolis: Winston, 1983); Thomas Oden's *Pastoral Theology* (San Francisco: Harper & Row, 1982).

1: WHOLENESS AND BEYOND

1. Morris L. West, *The Shoes of the Fisherman* (New York: William Morrow & Co., 1963), 254.
2. Carol Gilligan, *In A Different Voice* (Cambridge: Harvard University Press, 1982).
3. Gabriel Moran, *Religious Education Development: Images for the Future* (Minneapolis: Winston, 1983) 36.
4. John A. T. Robinson, *Truth is Two-Eyed* (Philadelphia: Westminster, 1979), 4–17.
5. Flannery O'Connor, *Habit of Being*, ed. Sally Fitzgerald (New York: Farrar, Straus & Giroux, 1979), 72.
6. Walker Percy, *The Second Coming* (New York: Farrar, Straus & Giroux, 1980), 401.

2: THE ROOTS OF HOLINESS

1. Eric James, "Holiness," in Gordon S. Wakefield, ed., *Dictionary of Christian Spirituality* (London: SCM Press, 1983), 245–47.
2. Bernard Brandon Scott, *Jesus, Symbol Maker for the Kingdom* (Philadelphia: Fortress Press, 1981), 25–32.
3. Scott, *Jesus*, 6.
4. Neil Richardson, *The Panorama of Luke* (London: Epworth Press, 1982), 23.
5. Thomas Hoyt, *The Poor in Luke—Acts*, quoted in Walter E. Pilgrim, *Good News to the Poor* (Minneapolis: Augsburg, 1981), 160.
6. Richardson, *The Panorama of Luke*, 31.

3: THE HOLY PERSON IN CONTEMPORARY SOCIETY

1. Martin Marty, "A Time-Capsule Report for the Year 2000," in *Context* 17, No. 1 (January 1, 1985).

2. Margaret Dewey, "The Quest for Wholeness," *Thinking Mission* (Autumn 1984), No. 44 (London: The United Society for the Proclamation of the Gospel).
3. John Carmody, *Holistic Spirituality* (New York: Paulist Press, 1983), 135.
4. André Dubus, "A Father's Story," in John Updike, ed., *The Best American Short Stories, 1984* (Boston: Houghton Mifflin, 1984), 78.

4: PASTORAL DIMENSIONS OF HOLINESS

1. Brother Fidelis of Mary, FSC, "Design for Holiness," *Cross and Crown* 17 (1965): 60–61.
2. Henri J. M. Nouwen, Douglas A. Morrison, and Donald P. McNeil, *Compassion* (Garden City: Doubleday, 1982), 4.
3. D. M. Thomas, *The White Hotel* (New York: Viking Press, 1981). Quoted from Pocket Books edition, 321–22.
4. John Braine, *Room at the Top* (London: Penguin Books, 1959), 235.
5. Don Browning, *The Moral Context of Pastoral Care* (Philadelphia: Westminster, 1976), 100.
6. Gabriel Moran, *Religious Education Development: Images for the Future* (Minneapolis: Winston, 1983), 101.
7. Kenneth Leech, *The Social God* (London: Sheldon Press, 1981), 67.
8. Kenneth Leech, "Spiritual Direction and Soul Justice: Seven Theses," *PHOS Theological Reflections* (Published by the Trinity Institute of Trinity Church, New York, Advent 1982).

5: PRAYER AND THE KINGDOM VISION

1. Loren Eisley, *The Immense Journey* (New York: Time, 1962), p. 169.
2. Abraham Joshua Heschel's works are quoted in Leon Klenicki and Gabe Huck, *Spirituality and Prayer: Jewish and Christian Understandings* (New York: Paulist Press, 1983). I saw this first in Martin Marty's *Context* (March 15, 1984).
3. Segundo Galilea, "Politics and Contemplation: The Mystical and Political Dimensions of the Christian Faith," in *The Mystical and Political Dimensions of the Christian Faith*, Claude Geffre and Gustavo Gutierrez, ed. (New York: Herder & Herder, 1974), 28.
4. Elizabeth O'Connor, *Letters to Scattered Pilgrims* (San Francisco: Harper & Row, 1979), 108.
5. Frederick Buechner, *Godric* (New York: Atheneum, 1981), 142.
6. Henri J. M. Nouwen, *Reaching Out* (New York: Doubleday, 1979), 89.
7. Frederick Buechner, *The Sacred Journey* (San Francisco: Harper & Row, 1982), 107.

6: WORK, VOCATION, AND INTEGRITY

1. David Mamet, *Glengarry Glen Ross* (New York: Grove Press, 1982), 105.
2. Jacques Ellul, *The Ethics of Freedom*, Geoffrey W. Bromiley, trans. (Grand Rapids: Wm. B. Eerdman's, 1976), 507.

3. John Vogelsang, "Personality, Faith Development and Work Attitudes," *Journal of Religion and Health* 22, No. 2 (Summer 1983): 131–32.

4. Elizabeth O'Connor, *The New Community* (New York: Harper & Row, 1976), 58.

5. Frederick Buechner, *Wishful Thinking* (New York: Harper & Row, 1973), 95.

7: EDUCATION FOR HOLINESS

1. Thomas H. Groome, *Christian Religious Education* (San Francisco: Harper & Row, 1980), 25.

2. Mark Helprin, *Winter's Tale* (New York: Harcourt, Brace, Jovanovich, 1983), 172–73.

3. Anthony Padovano, "Aesthetic Experience and Redemptive Grace," in Gloria Durka and Joanmarie Smith, eds., *Aesthetic Dimensions of Religious Education* (New York: Paulist Press, 1979), 3.

4. Rainer Maria Rilke, *Letters to a Young Poet* (New York: W. W. Norton & Co., 1934), 35.

5. Henri J. M. Nouwen, *¡Gracias!* (San Francisco: Harper & Row, 1983), 31.

6. Frederick Buechner, *The Magnificent Defeat* (New York: Seabury Press, 1966), 124–25.

EPILOGUE: A MODERN PARABLE

1. See Chapter 1 and the reference to John A. T. Robinson's *Truth is Two-Eyed* (Philadelphia: Westminster, 1979).

2. Ruth Bornstein, *The Dancing Man* (New York: Seabury Press, 1978).

3. "Lord of the Dance" (Simple Gifts), Traditional Folk Hymn adapted by Sydney Carter.

Index

Acceptance in Christ, 87–88
"A Father's Story" (Dubus), 31

Baptism, 28, 68
Bartimaeus, 78
Baruch-Segel study, 70–71
Bible: holiness in, 15–16; *see also* New
  Testament
Bishops' pastoral on economy, 35
Bornstein, Ruth, 90–91
Braine, John, 45–46
Browning, Don, ix–x, 46
Buber, Martin, 32
Buechner, Frederick, 58, 61, 72, 83
Burning bush, 16

Call to holiness, 34, 36
Career and family, 70–71
Caring, ix
Carmody, John, 30
Center, finding of, 6–7
Characteristics of holiness, 32–33
Christ. *See* Jesus
Christian Religious Education (Groome),
  75
The Cloisters, 78
Community, person in, 72
Community of faith, 89
Companionship in Christ, 47–50
Compassion, 41–44
Contemplative vision, 55

The Dancing Man (Bornstein), 90–91
Death of a Salesman (Miller), 65
Dewey, Margaret, 30
Dubus, André, 31

Education, 75–83; in discipleship, 39
Eiseley, Loren, 55–56
Ellul, Jacques, 69
Enterprise Foundation, 66
Environment for holiness, 76–77
Erikson, Erik, 5
The Ethics of Freedom (Ellul), 69
Eucharistic liturgy, 82

Experience of God, 16

Faith, gift of, 9–12, 86–87
Family and work, 70–71
Fowler, James, 5
Freudian thought, 5

Galilea, Segundo, 56–57
Gandhi, Mahatma, 90
Gilligan, Carol, 5, 46
Glengarry Glen Ross (Mamet), 65
God: generosity of, 22; and Moses, 15–
  16; presence of, 49–50;
  reacquaintance with, 59; *see also*
  Kingdom of God
Godric (Buechner), 58
Good News, 60
Good Samaritan parable, 19–20
¡Gracias! (Nouwen), 81
Groome, Thomas, 75
Growing towards maturity, x

Helprin, Mark, 77–78
Heschel, Rabbi Abraham Joshua, 56
Holy worldliness, 30–31
Hoyt, Thomas, 22

Imagination, expanding of, 77–78
The Immense Journey (Eiseley), 55–56
Inner conflicts, 7
Inner life, 81–83
Integrity, 71–72
Intercessions, 82
Isaiah, 21
I-Thou experience, 32

James, Eric, 18
Jesus: acceptance in Christ, 87–88;
  companionship in Christ, 47–50;
  compassion of, 41–42; and John the
  Baptist, 60; and Kingdom of God,
  20–23; and Law of Moses, 45;
  parables of, 19–20; participation
  with, 18–19; testing beliefs, 7;
  vocation of, 71–72

John the Baptist, 60
Jung, Carl, 4, 5

King, Martin Luther, Jr., 57, 90
Kingdom of God, 19, 20–23; and holiness in, 10; working for, 89–90
Koenig, John, 44
Kohlberg, Lawrence, 5, 46

Law of Moses, 45
Leech, Kenneth, 48–49
Letters to a Young Poet (Rilke), 79
Life cycle issues, ix–x
Life questions, framing of, 79–80

The Magnificent Defeat (Buechner), 83
Mamet, David, 65
Marriage, covenant in, 8
Marty, Martin, 29–30, 34
Mary Magdalene, 42
May, Gerald, 47
Micah, 18
Miller, Arthur, 65
The Moral Context of Pastoral Care (Browning), 46
Moral guidance, 46
Moralism, 40
Moran, Gabriel, 6, 46–47
Moses, 15–16; Law of, 45
Movements in prayer, 57–58
Mutuality in ministry, 70

Neutral space, 32–33
New Testament: holiness in, 17; and pastoral care, 39; and righteousness, 44
Nouwen, Henri, 59, 81

O'Connor, Elizabeth, 57, 72
O'Connor, Flannery, 11
Old Testament, holiness in, 16–17

Padovano, Anthony, 78
Parables of Jesus, 19–20
Participation and holiness, 17–19
Pathway to holiness, 86–90
Paul, apostle, 7, 33; as activist, 57; and living Christ, 10; on transformation, 60
Percy, Walker, 11–12
"Personality, Faith Development, and

Work Attitudes" (Vogelsang), 70
Peter, apostle, 17
Piaget, Jean, 5
Polarization of the world, 35
Pontius Pilate, 21
Poor: housing for, 66; and rich, 22
Prayer, 55; in God, 59–60; as language of the Kingdom, 56; three movements in, 57–58; through God, 60–61; toward God, 58–59
Priestly tradition, 16–17
Principled non-violence, 46
Psychotherapy, 47

Questions for living, 79–80

Richardson, Neil, 21–22
Rich persons, 22
Right belief, 87
Righteousness, 44–47
Rilke, Rainer Maria, 79
Robinson, John A. T., 6, 87
Role of Church, 40–41
Roman Catholic Bishops' pastoral on economy, 35
Room at the Top (Braine), 45–46
Rouse, James, 66–67

The Sacred Journey (Buechner), 61
Sacred space, 16–17
Salvation, 4, 65
Scott, Bernard Brandon, 19–20
Scripture, surprises of, 78–79
The Second Coming (Percy), 11–12
The Self, 5
Self-actualization, x
Self-discovery, 7
Sensitivity of Jesus, 42
Servanthood, 72
Shoes of the Fisherman (West), 3
Simeon, 18
The Social God (Leech), 48–49
Solidarity with others, 88–89
Solitary hero, 3, 4
Soviet architecture, 66
Spirit, gifts of, 59
Spiritual direction, 48–49

Temple of Jerusalem, 16
Teresa of Calcutta, Mother, 34, 57, 90
Terrorism, 35

Thomas, D. M., 43
Thomas, Lewis, 30
Transformation, 10, 60
Tribalism, 29
Truth, 5
Tutu, Desmond, 27–28, 32, 90

Vision of holiness, ix
Vocation, 67–72
Vogelsang, John, 70
Voluntary displacement, 80–81

West, Morris, 3
The White Hotel (Thomas), 43
Wholeness, quest for, x, xi, 3–6
Winter's Tale (Helprin), 77–78
Work and family, 70–71
Worldly holiness, 30–31
Worship, 31, 81–83

Zacchaeus, 21, 42